Praise for *What You're Really Meant to Do*

"Rob Kaplan has written a very insightful book based on the important but often neglected premise that the key to realizing your unique potential—and thereby living a fulfilling professional life—is to create your own definition of success rather than accept the definition created by others. Kaplan offers inspirational and practical advice on choosing a professional path that is right for you and provides a series of disciplined steps to help you succeed to your fullest potential. This book will be invaluable reading for students deciding on what careers to pursue and for the far too many people who are dissatisfied in the jobs they now hold."

—Ira Magaziner, Vice Chairman and CEO, Clinton Health Access Initiative; Chairman, Clinton Clean Energy Initiative

"A valuable road map by someone who's been there and done it successfully. Rob Kaplan's unique approach offers some very practical and actionable steps that any aspiring leader can, and should, put into play."

—Art Gingold, Executive Coach

"This book is not about how to achieve specific outcomes; it is about creating a sustainable path to personal growth and fulfillment. It focuses on helping you pursue your intrinsic motivations, such as exploring intellectual challenges, creating strong interpersonal relationships, making a positive impact on the world, and solving problems that are meaningful to you."

—R. C. Buford, President, Sports Franchises; General Manager, San Antonio Spurs

"This book is inspiring and a reminder that in life you need to be willing to take risks and not be afraid to be an x among the o's. Rob Kaplan has lived what he has written so he has had a unique vantage point on these life lessons. His perspective is one that we can all benefit from."

—Caryn Seidman-Becker, Chairman and CEO, CLEAR

WHAT
YOU'RE
REALLY
MEANT
TO DO

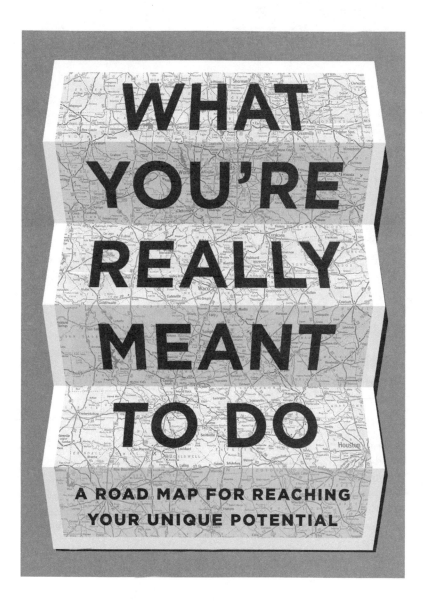

WHAT YOU'RE REALLY MEANT TO DO

A ROAD MAP FOR REACHING YOUR UNIQUE POTENTIAL

ROBERT STEVEN KAPLAN

Harvard Business Review Press • Boston, Massachusetts

No part of this publication may be reproduced, stored in or introduced into a retrieval system, or transmitted, in any form, or by any means (electronic, mechanical, photocopying, recording, or otherwise), without the prior permission of the publisher. Requests for permission should be directed to permissions@hbsp.harvard.edu, or mailed to Permissions, Harvard Business School Publishing, 60 Harvard Way, Boston, Massachusetts 02163.

The web addresses referenced in this book were live and correct at the time of the book's publication but may be subject to change.

Library of Congress Cataloging-in-Publication Data

Kaplan, Robert Steven.
    What you're really meant to do : a road map for reaching your unique potential/Robert Steven Kaplan.
        pages cm
    ISBN 978-1-4221-8990-0 (alk. paper)
    1. Career development.   2. Vocational guidance.   3. Job satisfaction.
I. Title.
    HF5381.K357 2013
    650.1–dc23   2012047090

The paper used in this publication meets the requirements of the American National Standard for Permanence of Paper for Publications and Documents in Libraries and Archives Z39.48-1992.

ISBN13: 978-1-4221-8990-0
eISBN: 978-1-4221-8991-7

To my parents, who always encouraged me to pursue my dreams

Contents

Contents

WHAT YOU'RE REALLY MEANT TO DO

Introduction

Reaching Your Unique Potential

This above all: to thine own self be true

—HAMLET

What does it mean to be "successful"? How do you achieve your dreams?

Does it mean creating an impressive list of achievements? Does it mean gaining significant wealth, status, position, and power? Maybe it means pleasing your parents, family, and friends?

I wrote this book to address these questions and to create a road map to help you achieve your aspirations. Following this road map involves taking a series of steps and answering a set of questions, all of which require you to look inward as well as outward. It also involves developing a set of new skills and habits, some of which may be challenging and uncomfortable for you.

Another Path

Having wrestled with these issues over the past thirty years, I have come to believe that the key to achieving your aspirations lies not in "being a success" but rather in *working to reach your unique potential.* This requires you to create your own definition of success rather than accept a definition created by others.

For many of us, navigating this road is very challenging because it forces us to understand ourselves and screen out many of the external forces that profoundly impact how we think about our careers and our lives. This path may also require you to develop a thick skin that enables you to ward off the polite ambivalence (or active disapproval) of those loved ones, friends, and colleagues who turn up their noses at certain choices you decide to make.

This book describes a different—and, I believe, ultimately more fulfilling—path. It is based on many of my own career and life experiences, as well as lessons I've learned in managing and advising a diverse range of people regarding how to reach their unique potential.

This approach takes courage and hard work. It does not yield easy answers or get you to a final destination. It is, instead, a multistage, lifelong effort. It involves developing a different mind-set and a new set of work habits.

I first started speaking about this subject when I was running businesses in the financial services industry. Over two decades, I led a number of businesses in a variety of geographic regions of the world. I dealt with a significant number of challenging situations and managed and advised a wide range of people. These experiences helped me develop deeper insight into the role of leadership, individual development, and the nature of human potential.

When I joined the faculty at Harvard in fall 2005, I began thinking more systemically about these issues as well as teaching many of these concepts. I wrote an article on this topic in the July–August 2008 edition of *Harvard Business Review*. I regularly receive phone calls, e-mails, and visits from people who have read it and want to discuss how it might apply to them.

Over the years, I have advised numerous students and executives, and I have consistently observed that great companies and nonprofit organizations create an environment in which people are coached and encouraged to reach their unique potential.

In 2009, I began to teach an HBS course titled "The Authentic Leader."[1] This course was created by former Medtronic CEO Bill George based on his superb book *True North*.[2] This experience further shaped my thinking and added a new dimension to my leadership activities and advice.

Each of Us Is Unique

Each of us has unique skills and qualities that we bring to any situation. We have different life stories, strengths and weaknesses, passions, anxieties, and idiosyncrasies. Consequently, doesn't it make sense that the ideal path would be somewhat different for each of us? Why, then, do we often try to mimic others and shoehorn ourselves into a cookie-cutter definition of success?

Think of people you know who have chosen their own individual paths. Perhaps they have started their own business, embarked on a career that appears to have little potential to be lucrative, joined a nonprofit endeavor, or otherwise made a career choice that flies in the face of current conceptions of what is "hot" or "cool."

Many of these people are not famous. Others, such as Steve Jobs and Bill Gates, are celebrated on the covers of business magazines as enormous successes even though no one was cheering them on when they dropped out of college and started working in their garages.

Why did these people have the courage to choose the paths they did? Were they so talented that they would naturally have been wildly successful, no matter what course they chose? Or did they develop specific habits and a mind-set that helped them follow their own drummer?

What You're Really Meant to Do

I believe there is a mind-set you can adopt and specific actions you can take that will help you realize your unique dreams. There are habits you can practice that will help you understand yourself better, improve your capabilities, and follow your own convictions. There are specific approaches that are useful to consider as you develop your life and career.

This book is not intended to help you attain material wealth, status, or power. It is not designed to help you figure out how to become celebrated as a "winner." It is, instead, a book about self-discovery. It is intended to help you better understand your skills, discover who you are, and define what you want. It is designed to help you develop strategies for navigating your life and career. This book describes a systematic approach for thinking and learning so that you improve your chances of reaching your own unique potential.

The following chapters describe a disciplined process. This process is not touchy-feely, and it avoids generalized answers or easy solutions. It is not intended to take the place of getting help from a psychiatrist, psychologist, or other mental health professional (something I strongly encourage if you believe you could benefit from this kind of help). Instead, it's about helping you strengthen your existing self-development muscles and build new ones.

Some of the lessons in this book can be learned and applied immediately; others may take years to internalize and apply. The key to this effort is not trying to arrive at a specific destination or establish a particular timetable. Instead, it is about learning how to develop your own path.

Reaching Your Potential

As with my last book, *What to Ask the Person in the Mirror,* this book encourages you to ask yourself a series of questions and perform a number of exercises.

My earlier book deals with questions that can help you become a more effective leader and improve your organization. This book is about asking questions and taking actions that will help you understand yourself and reach your unique potential. Again, it is not aimed at helping you make more money, achieve more status, or acquire more power—although I would strongly argue that these outcomes are ultimately more likely to occur if you follow this path. Rather, this book

FIGURE I-1

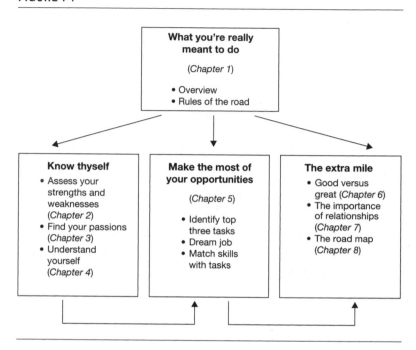

is about creating a sustainable path to personal growth and fulfillment.

The book is organized into eight chapters based on the framework shown in figure I-1. The chapters are as follows:

Chapter 1, What You're Really Meant to Do. In this chapter I lay out the premise for reaching your potential. I also propose rules of the road, which are essential to developing a mind-set that will help you to address each segment of this book and ultimately put its ideas into action. As with any long journey, it's helpful to get started with the right frame of mind. The advice in this book may be mechanically easy to follow, but internalizing these steps will likely require you to reexamine your presumptions and attitudes. Making this leap is challenging and can take time.

Chapter 2, Assessing Your Strengths and Weaknesses. This might sound easy enough, but some people are surprised by how difficult it is for them. A high percentage of people I speak with don't have a clear sense of their core strengths. At the same time, most people I talk with cannot accurately describe their weaknesses. This chapter challenges you to identify your own strengths and weaknesses. It discusses how to go about doing this and explains how to create a process for continually reassessing your skills for the rest of your life.

The chapter suggests several potential strategies for addressing and managing your strengths and weaknesses. I examine the role of coaching and explore why it is necessary to risk some degree of vulnerability in order to get a better handle on your skills.

Chapter 3, Finding Your Passions. What tasks do you really enjoy? How do you figure this out? What does passion have to do with career success? Can you really create a productive career doing something you love? Should you follow your passions now, or wait until you have made some money? How do your talents fit with your passions?

Many people struggle with figuring out their passions. This is particularly true if they're in a job they don't truly enjoy. This struggle can create a vicious cycle: lack of passion for your job limits your upward mobility, meaning that you're more likely to be stuck in that job indefinitely. It is difficult to become superb at a job you dislike. In this chapter, I discuss techniques to help you identify what you truly love, and I explore how to translate that passion into potential jobs and careers. Having passion helps you work on developing your strengths, addressing your weaknesses, and overcoming the many frustrations and obstacles you will face in developing your career.

Warren Buffett started with a simple passion: picking stocks. He ran a small investment fund for many years. He built on his strengths to become an outstanding CEO and build a superb company. He used his initial strengths to develop new strengths and was willing to learn new skills because he enjoyed his job.

Chapter 4, Understanding Yourself. What is your life story? Are you aware of the negative narratives in your head that may be hindering your performance? Do you feel blocked from taking certain actions that you know you need to take? This chapter discusses the challenge of identifying your blind spots and explains the need to understand why you do what you do. Understanding yourself is profoundly important to the quality of your choices in life. The most important person you will have to learn to manage is yourself.

Chapter 5, Making the Most of Your Opportunities. This chapter discusses how to match your strengths, weaknesses, passions, and understanding of who you are, with being effective in your current or a prospective job. It explores the importance of doing enough analysis and inquiry to identify the three most important tasks that are critical to your job. Do you know what they are? Can you write them down? Do you enjoy those tasks? Do you spend time on them? Do you gear your skill development to improving your ability to execute these tasks?

Reaching your potential requires you to make wise choices about how to spend your time. It requires you to choose an industry, job function, and company to pursue. Turning down the wrong job is just as important as choosing the right one. This choice is particularly difficult if you are highly motivated by money, status, and the opinions of others, or if you have an unclear sense of your passions and your skills. You need to put yourself in a position where you have an opportunity to shine.

Chapter 6, Good Versus Great. This chapter is about the critical intangibles that, over time, will increasingly determine whether you reach your full potential. It is about your mind-set and behaviors. It discusses the benefits of choosing to do for others without regard to what's in it for you—acting as an owner. It discusses the importance of believing that justice will prevail. I also explore the issue of playing it safe—for example, being too politically correct and failing to speak up, express your opinions, and even make waves as appropriate. The failure to articulate strongly held views, set ethical boundaries, and speak truth to power can lead promising professionals to underperform and can limit their career prospects.

Chapter 7, The Importance of Relationships. Reaching your potential is not a journey you can take all by yourself. At many points in your career, you will need the assistance of others. Again, creating relationships is harder than it sounds. Many of us believe we are tightly connected to others and we have strong relationships to call on—until that moment when we are under stress and looking for help. Then we realize that we haven't cultivated critical relationships with people who could help us with feedback and advice.

It is critical to develop relationships with people who care enough about you to tell you the brutal truth—things you need to hear even though you don't want to hear them. These people care enough about you to risk you being upset with them. They can serve as a powerful reality check.

I am constantly struck by how isolated people are, despite being hyperconnected on Facebook or closely followed on Twitter. In my experience, one of the key impediments to reaching our potential is isolation. We all have blind spots. Sooner or later, we all need to reach out for help and reveal some degree of our vulnerability.

I speak from experience. For many years, I was deathly afraid of speaking in front of large crowds. I was convinced that I couldn't do it, and I was embarrassed to admit this fear to my peers or bosses. I went so far as to turn down promotions, knowing that if I took a bigger job, I would have to address large audiences regularly. I finally worked up the courage to confess this fear to a close associate. As a result of this discussion, I began to work on developing techniques for learning to speak effectively to a crowd. In my case, it turned out that focusing on speaking from the heart—about what I truly believed—was a way of overcoming my fear. I needed help from others, however, before I could begin to figure this out.

Do you have a handful of trusted colleagues or friends—even one or two—who care about you enough to listen, understand you, and give you feedback you need to hear? These people don't need to be your "best friends," but they do need to be people you trust and can confide in. This chapter discusses how learning to play this role for others is often an excellent way to better understand yourself and at the same time become more adept at cultivating close relationships with others.

Chapter 8, The Road Map. What helps you follow the prescriptions in this book? What hinders you? How do you overcome these impediments? How do short-term money problems and other crises impact this journey? This chapter will help you put the core ideas of this book into a sustainable process, using its exercises and other tools to help you bring it all together.

The Road Ahead

There's no single right way to accomplish your goals. Each of us has a number of avenues to reach our potential. The world constantly changes. Life often unfolds as a series of phases. Our potential is likely to evolve as the world evolves and as we continue to learn, grow, and develop our capabilities.

Reaching your potential is not simply about dreaming or being idealistic. It is a process that involves specific actions, exercises, discipline, and hard work. It is challenging, rewarding, and unending. I believe you will find that it's worth it and, in the long run, this process will help you to experience a much greater level of satisfaction and fulfillment in your life and career.

CHAPTER ONE

What You're Really Meant to Do

Getting Started

- What is your definition of success?
- What steps will you take to achieve your aspirations?

One of the best aspects of my job is having the opportunity to talk with business people, nonprofit leaders, and students who want to discuss sensitive issues of importance to them. Our conversations often turn to what they can do to achieve their dreams and reach their potential. Their backgrounds, stories, and specific situations differ, but all of these people share some degree of frustration and confusion about how to find meaning and make the most of their lives.

In this opening chapter, I recount a few of these stories—as well as examples from my own life—and introduce the idea that you can take ownership of defining your own success and achieving your unique potential. To help you tackle this challenge, I propose five rules of the road. They're intended to get you in the right frame of mind and make this book more useful to you.

Getting Started: The Initial Career Choice

An accomplished graduate student was fortunate to have received full-time job offers from various financial services firms. He knew that I had previously spent my career in that industry, so he asked my advice about which firm to join.

I responded to his initial questions by asking him which firm he thought he might enjoy most. He wasn't sure. "Actually, I'm kind of ambivalent about all of these jobs," he said. "I know I should be excited. My classmates would kill for some of these offers."

Given his admission, I asked him why he wanted to work in this business.

"I think I can do the job for a few years," he said. "I've got significant student loans, and my parents have struggled financially their entire lives. Any one of these jobs would help me begin to reduce my loans and eventually help my folks."

As we talked, he asked me which job I would take. I suggested that my choice probably wouldn't help him figure out what *he* should do. Then I asked him whether he had a passion for the financial markets. His answer was immediate and unequivocal: "No."

"Do you have a passion for the key tasks that are likely to be critical in any of these jobs?"

"I'm not sure," he said, "but I am concerned that the answer is no."

I then asked an obvious question: "So, if you don't like the markets and you question whether you'll enjoy what you'd be doing each day at one of these firms, are you sure you're looking in the right industry?"

He sat silently.

"OK," I continued. "Let me ask you this. What would you do if money weren't a consideration? Let's say you got a big inheritance from a rich uncle. What would you do under *those* circumstances?"

"That's easy," he responded with a smile. "I wouldn't take *any* of these jobs. I'm a musician, a classical pianist. I *love* music. I would try to get a job at a record company or in some other business aspect of the music industry."

"Wow," I said. "If that's the case, why aren't you pursuing those types of jobs *now*? You're thirty years old! When do you think you're going to pursue this passion, if not soon? Is it really going to be that easy to move to a dramatically different industry three to five years from now?"

He explained that he had pursued the hot jobs during the recruiting season at his school. Although salary and potential bonuses were a consideration, he also mentioned that his friends thought it was really cool that he was going to work in financial services. These were highly sought-after jobs, he emphasized, sounding as if he was trying to convince himself.

We spent the rest of the meeting further discussing the specific trade-off decisions he was facing, identifying whom he was trying to please, and deciding what factors were truly important to him. We also discussed whether there were alternative actions he might take, in addition to his job choice, that would allow him to continue to pursue his ultimate dream.

Midcareer: Stuck in No-Man's-Land

A day later, a forty-one-year-old sales manager from the Midwest came to visit me in Boston. A mutual friend had asked me to talk with him. After we briefly got acquainted, he asked if he could shut my office door. He then sat back down on my couch and made a confession: "I think I'm in a lot of trouble."

"What kind of trouble?"

"I think I've hit a wall. I've made some huge mistakes."

"OK, what kind of mistakes?"

"Well, I'm not sure how to explain it," he said. "Certainly I've made a pretty good living. My parents, friends, and family think I'm a success. I guess I have a career that other people might envy. I have a great wife and three great kids. I've got a nice house and some money in the bank. We're not extravagant and are careful about unnecessary spending. I am working on saving enough to pay for the kids' college and retire at sixty-five or seventy."

"Sounds great," I said. "So what's the problem?"

He hesitated. "I guess I feel stupid to be taking up your time. I know you're not a psychiatrist. Maybe there *isn't* any problem. But it's just that I don't feel good about myself. I'm not sure what I'm accomplishing, and I don't feel the satisfaction I think I should be experiencing. Other than my marriage and kids, I don't feel like any of what I'm doing is important. I don't have great passion for selling my firm's product, and I think my performance is deteriorating—for example, I was recently passed over for a promotion to vice president.

"I thought that at this point in my career, I would be reaching my peak performance and feeling very energized about my job, but I don't. Is it too late to switch to a job I'm better suited for? How do I even go about thinking about this? Is this what midcareer feels like? Is this what success feels like?"

He had invoked the magic word: "success." What *is* success, and how is it supposed to feel?

I suggested we take a big step back. I asked him to tell me more about his life and about how he wound up in his current job. We discussed what he did and didn't enjoy in his job. I asked him about his strengths and weaknesses and his passions. He hadn't thought much about these questions, and we agreed he'd need to consider them more after he left my office. We discussed what success meant to him, as opposed to what it meant to his friends, family, and those around him.

I asked him who else he had discussed these issues with. "Nobody," he replied.

I told him that I could understand being reluctant to confide in one's coworkers, and maybe even in certain friends who might not understand. But surely he must have someone he could confide in?

"No," he said firmly. "My friends wouldn't get it—and some might be privately pleased that I'm having problems. I don't want to burden my wife and other loved ones. They might worry I'm not doing as well as they thought, and I don't want that. My sisters are having financial troubles, and I don't think they'd be terribly sympathetic to what might sound like a self-indulgent psychodrama."

We concluded the discussion by outlining a series of questions and issues for him to consider that might help him make sense of the situation and help him begin to figure out what to do next.

Who Defines Your Success?

I've been having these types of conversations for the past twenty-five years. They started when I first began managing people. On a regular basis, a colleague or client would visit me, close the door, and make more or less the same kind of confession: "By any reasonable measure, I'm doing fine, but it doesn't mean what I thought it would mean. I thought I would have achieved more and be hitting my stride by now. I thought I would be happier; I'm really not enjoying myself." Very often, these statements were made with urgency and evident distress. The conversation sometimes came on the heels of a big promotion or, conversely, during a period when the person's career was languishing.

Often, the person would say things like, "I want to accomplish more. I think I am capable of so much more. I want to achieve something significant. I don't want to explain to my grandchildren that my entire life boiled down to a set of transactions, client triumphs, earnings reports, or simply a paycheck."

I noticed a common thread: many of these people were surprised to discover that monetary rewards were insufficient to sustain them in their careers. It turned out that money was not the powerful or consistent motivator they thought it would be.

After a great many of these discussions, I began to wonder why so many highly capable people were dissatisfied, felt as if they were underachieving, or were unfulfilled in their professional careers and in their lives. I empathized with them because, at times, I had experienced some of the same feelings. I had also been raised to believe that monetary rewards and professional accomplishments made people happier. Yet many of the people I was speaking with were describing a feeling of emptiness despite some level of material success and impressive professional credentials.

What were they missing? And did the answer to that question extend to me as well? Was I missing something in the way I thought about my career and life?

When I came to Harvard to teach in 2005, I continued to have these discussions, but on a much broader scale. I saw this phenomenon play out in people from different cultures, countries, industries, socioeconomic levels, and professions. In young people, it manifested itself in a struggle to develop skills, achieve some measure of self-awareness, and make wise choices about a future career. In midcareer executives, it was more likely to be reflected in a feeling of confusion about where to turn and a concern that they had painted themselves into a corner. In older executives and professionals, it was sometimes reflected in feelings of outright regret and bitterness.

In almost all cases, these people were beginning to resent the expectations of others and were trying to come to a more accurate assessment of their skills, their dreams, and their true desires as human beings. They had listened to what the world encouraged them to do, and they had worked hard to meet those expectations. Their concerns were thrown into sharp relief when they encountered peers who had not attained the same level of material wealth as they but who appeared far happier, truer to their values and beliefs, more challenged in their work, and more passionate and fulfilled in their careers and lives.

These situations resonate deeply with me because I have struggled with these same issues. As a result, over the years, I have become increasingly convinced that the way we have been conditioned to think about our lives and careers may ultimately cause us to be confused about our passions, skill-development needs, and critical choices. We are susceptible to pursuing paths that are based on someone else's compass rather than our own.

Who Sets Your Benchmarks?

When I was growing up, my parents often talked to me about the importance of working hard and becoming successful. "You should go into a profession," they would say. "Doctor, dentist, lawyer are all good professions. Orthodontists also do very well!"

My parents justifiably believed that professional status would allow me to have a better life than they had. They grew up during the Depression, and both began working at young ages to help support their families. They both continued to work long hours throughout their adult lives. My father traveled extensively as a jewelry salesman in the Midwest, and my mother was a real estate agent who took on other work as money needs arose.

They both hoped that I wouldn't have to deal with the financial stresses they had faced. They wanted me to have a nest egg. They hoped I would achieve professional success and social status. Like most parents, they wanted to be proud of me and wanted to feel confident they had launched me on the road to a better life.

Although most of us grow up as products of our families, we are also heavily influenced by the social norms manifested in popular culture. I had a pretty typical upbringing. I watched a lot of television and read popular magazines. I was influenced by the media, which regularly celebrated "winners." Just as they are today, the winners were usually described as those who had made a lot of money and attained wealth, power, or influence. I read the advertisements and magazine covers, which were dominated by the smiling faces of people who had "made it." Boy, they sure seemed happy!

As a student, I was regularly assessed, tested, graded, and otherwise measured against "objective" metrics. As is true for most of us who grew up in the latter half of the twentieth century, the first twenty-two years of my life seemed to revolve around an unending series of tests designed to rank me versus my peer group. At the end of each grading period, my mom would ask me if I had made the honor roll. She was disappointed in me if I hadn't—not a good feeling! I internalized these standards and began to believe that academic metrics and accomplishments would be critical in determining where I could go to college and the kinds of jobs I would be able to get after college. To the extent that I thought about it, I figured I would eventually focus on what I wanted and who I was—but, for now, if I wanted to take the next step up the ladder, I needed to excel at what I was doing.

Later, when it came time to pick a job and career, I asked my parents and friends for advice. I didn't fully understand what was involved in various types of careers, so I wasn't really sure what I would like. As a result, I gravitated toward those jobs that everyone else seemed to want. If everybody else wanted certain jobs, I thought, they must be worth pursuing. Once I was actually in a job, I focused intently on how to excel at it so that I could be in a position to get a good review and be promoted. I certainly did not want to have to explain at a cocktail party why I had been passed over for a promotion.

Although I'm exaggerating this narrative a bit to make a point, I do think that many of us are trained to dream of success in terms of benchmarks, accomplishments, and milestones. At the same time, we are trained to fear the stigma of failing to achieve these critical metrics. Many of us are encouraged to focus more on *extrinsic* motivators—those that can be manifested visibly (money, status, title, etc.)—as opposed to *intrinsic* motivators, which are those things that motivate us internally (such as passion for the mission, intellectual stimulation, and close relationships).

Do You Take Ownership of Selecting Your Own Path?

Many of us motor through our young adult years trying to rack up one achievement after another—being "successful"—without thinking through what we truly want. At many points along this journey, we seek or get guidance from well-meaning peers, friends, family, and loved ones who advise us what we should desire and what we should avoid. Little of this advice is based on any deep understanding of who we are as individuals, but rather on the advice givers' own experiences, desires, and understanding of social norms.

Fortunately, some young people get the kind of wise guidance and coaching that help them focus at an early stage on their strengths, weaknesses, passions, and sense of self. Others gain this insight later in life, perhaps with the help of mentors and other people with whom they have strong relationships and who take the time to understand them as individuals. With this support, they develop the strength, confidence, and self-awareness to gravitate toward paths that fit their passions and skills.

As discussed earlier, over my career I have spoken with and advised a steady stream of young, middle-, and later-stage professionals who excelled for a period but then began to struggle professionally and to experience doubt about what they wanted. In the early stages of their careers, they have the opportunity to develop new habits and make choices that will get them on the right track. At later stages, it is still not too late, although they may feel that they've "accomplished" their way into a dilemma: a life that looks good to others but doesn't tap their true capabilities or fulfill their passions and desires. They regret that they waited too long to develop good habits for honing their skills or for thinking deeply about what they wanted.

Does any of this sound like you? Are you making the most of your capabilities? Do you feel as if you're on someone else's path? If so, is it too late to make changes? Is there another way to manage your life and career and climb the next mountain?

Five Suggested Rules of the Road

The following chapters lay out a step-by-step road map for reaching your unique potential. Your chances of success on this journey will be greatly enhanced if you are able to develop a certain mind-set. To help you do this, I suggest here some general rules of the road that I reference throughout this book.

Believe That Justice Will Prevail

At some point in our lives, each of us has been treated unfairly. For example, most of us have received speeding tickets that we believe we didn't deserve. Perhaps you were passed over for a promotion you believed you had earned. Maybe you were misjudged by someone. Each of us can probably catalog a list of injustices, small and large, that we feel have been perpetrated upon us.

Those people who accumulate a sufficiently long list of perceived injustices often come to question the basic fairness of their company, the business world, and society in general.

As a result of these experiences, they decide that they won't do something unless they're certain they'll get something back in return. They become gun-shy about sticking their necks out, listening to their natural instincts, or helping others.

In my experience, if you fall into this mind-set, it ultimately diverts you from focusing on who you are and what you truly believe. It distracts you from figuring out what issues are truly important to you. It dissuades you from taking sensible risks and extending a helping hand to others.

If you want to reach your potential, you must be willing to figure out what you believe and have the courage to act on your beliefs. You need to make a leap of faith that, even though justice may not prevail at a given point in time, ultimately it will prevail. I believe that if you have this mind-set, you will perform at a higher level and will increase the likelihood of ultimately making the most of your capabilities.

Taking the actions suggested in this book will be easier if you work on making this leap of faith. That is, even though you will experience injustice, if you are *true to yourself and your convictions,* eventually you will be treated fairly.

Why do I emphasize this concept so strongly? Consider the alternative. What happens if you don't believe justice will prevail? Simply put, you'll get jaded and cynical. When your cynicism persuades you to give up on your internal moorings and convictions, you start obsessing about pleasing other people and meeting their expectations. You get away from understanding yourself and knowing what you believe in—and you start to make poor decisions.

Beware of Conventional Wisdom

Conventional wisdom is, in a nutshell, the prevailing views of others. It is commonly accepted wisdom. It's what the "smart folks" think. Although this wisdom is all around us, it is frequently dead wrong—particularly as it relates to you. It tends to be backward looking, and it fails to take into account your distinctive attributes and experience.

Unfortunately, conventional wisdom and peer pressure are pervasive. They manifest themselves in the commonly held views of family, friends, classmates, work colleagues, and folks you meet at cocktail receptions, and extend to television programs, commercials, billboards, and articles in print media. Conventional wisdom is so ubiquitous that we are often unaware of the powerful impact it can have on our thinking.

Think about all those messages we receive that claim to be the inside scoop on how to get ahead. They tend to take the form: *everybody knows that you need to do such and such in order to accomplish so and so*. Everyone knows that home prices never go down. Everyone knows that stocks will outperform bonds. Everyone knows that if you become a doctor, you can write your own ticket.

As you've undoubtedly seen, promising young people often go into professions because "everyone knows" that's the hot career. Unfortunately, you are the one who must actually live with the consequences of choices you make on the basis of conventional wisdom and peer pressure. What is hot today may not look so hot tomorrow, or it may not be a good fit with your skills and interests. The world changes, you change, and social views change. Even worse, conventional wisdom simply can't take into account who *you* are and what you're truly capable of.

In my experience, listening to peers and heeding conventional wisdom are often ways we punt on the tougher job of figuring out our interests and in what careers we might flourish. Beware of conventional wisdom, and focus instead on the difficult task of understanding who you are and where your interests lie. The answers may surprise you.

Act Like an Owner of Your Life and Your Choices

Managing your life and your career is 100 percent your responsibility. Do you act like it?

You are not a passive bystander in your own life. Many of the lessons and exercises in this book require you to do a substantial amount of independent thinking and soul-searching. Like getting into shape physically, you need to do exercises. Just as you must "own" the challenge of physical fitness—no one else can do it for you—you must own the responsibility for developing your skills, understanding yourself, and making critical choices. Yes, good organizations may help employees with this challenge, but you can't count on that.

Acting like an owner means taking responsibility for learning about your strengths, weaknesses, and passions. It involves communicating your desires to those who can help you achieve them. It means you own your fate.

It means you try to make your choices explicit. There are always trade-offs to be weighed, and you should try to make them explicit whenever possible. You should not passively wait for someone else to give you feedback or tell you what you should want or do. Your life is your responsibility. If you make mistakes, figure out what you could do better next time. You are not a victim. You are the proactive driver of your own life.

Be Realistic and Adapt to Circumstances

Some people say to me, "I would like to follow many of the prescriptions you discuss, but my main concern right now is paying this month's rent!" OK, fair enough. If you've just lost your job, or if you're struggling to make ends meet, you must make compromises. My father couldn't always pursue his professional desires because he had to deal with tough economic realities while we were growing up. Later, after he had heart bypass surgery, he had to make further compromises. If the economy is lousy, or if you or a loved one is suffering from a severe medical condition, you must take those constraints into account. If the barn is burning down, you must make putting out the fire your top priority.

Yet you can't let day-to-day setbacks—even major ones—knock you completely off the path of reaching your potential. Constantly fighting fires can become a way of life, and constantly dealing with short-term crises can create a vicious cycle.

This book discusses the importance of the clock in your head. Part of being realistic is operating on multiple time frames: dealing with today's crisis and, at the same time, planting seeds

today that will allow you to develop your potential in more fa-
vorable times and circumstances.

Be Open to Learning

If you're open to learning and to changing your behavior, you
have a terrific chance to reach your potential.[2] It is critical that
you be motivated to learn, change, and go further in your life.
This can be much harder than it sounds. Most people believe
they are open to learning, but when it becomes necessary, they
are slow to engage in meaningful introspection. They are reluctant to solicit feedback—and may even send out a vibe that
they really don't want advice.

Some people, especially as they become more senior, think
they are supposed to know all the answers, and they feel deeply
insecure and uncomfortable if they don't. They feel embarrassed to acknowledge they don't know what they should be
doing or that they need to improve and learn. Some people
don't feel comfortable admitting they have made a mistake or
have changed their minds. Some people see it as a sign of weakness to ask for advice. Others simply have shut down their
openness to new information and change—and, even though
they may not be aware of it, those around them see it clearly.

You must be motivated to learn in order to tackle many of
the assignments outlined in the following chapters. Some of the
suggested actions will likely make you feel awkward and uncomfortable. This disquiet may be a good thing if it causes you
to examine why you are uncomfortable in a particular situation
and to take steps to overcome your discomfort.

experience, all this is challenging but doable, if you're
to learn. If you are open and willing, this book will
help you aim higher—and, ultimately, go farther.

This chapter lays out the premise of this approach and explains
key rules of the road for embarking on this trip. The next few
chapters directly address the fundamental steps and road map
for reaching your potential.

Suggested Follow-Up Steps

- Write down your definition of success.
- Write down the steps you believe you will need to take
  to achieve your dreams.
- Keep these answers in a notebook. You might revisit
  and update your thinking as you go through each chapter of this book.

CHAPTER TWO

Assessing Your Strengths and Weaknesses

Own the Process of Developing Your Capabilities

- Can you write down your three most significant skill-based strengths and your three most significant weaknesses?
- What are the top three capabilities required for your current job or for a prospective job?
- Do you own the responsibility for assessing your skills, evaluating them in relation to job requirements, and seeking out coaches?

I have worked with many successful people who have put immense energy into learning how to assess their strengths and weaknesses. It did not come easily to most of them, but they made a tremendous effort to get better at this because they realized it could make a huge difference in their careers and lives. They understood that the effort to reach their unique potential begins with a fundamental understanding of strengths and weaknesses.

In my experience, the reason people often fail to grow and improve isn't necessarily that they lack the ability. Instead, they lack awareness of their skills and skill deficiencies. I have been consistently impressed with the capacity of people to build their capabilities once they identify the skills they need to improve. The key is awareness of, and then motivation to address, their weaknesses. People can make enormous progress once they've accepted responsibility for this challenge.

Understanding your strengths and your weaknesses is not a mechanical exercise. It requires you to follow a sequence of steps that involve intense focus and concentration on your part, and solid advice from others who observe you. To improve your skills, you need to be receptive to constructive criticism and open to feeling uncomfortable.

Are You Motivated to Improve?

This chapter will discuss how you can go about better understanding your strengths and weaknesses. I outline how you can create a process for doing this regularly so that you can update and adapt your thinking to new jobs and new circumstances. I explain the impediments that stand in the way of doing this difficult work. Some of these obstacles may be apparent to you, but others may be less obvious. We will explore various avenues for addressing these impediments.

This chapter examines the essential role of getting coaching. It attempts to dispel several misconceptions you may have regarding coaching and addresses how you can take greater ownership of the coaching process.

Once you have solicited coaching and are armed with a greater awareness of your skills, what strategies should you pursue for building your career? Should you focus more on strengths? Should you seek jobs that play to your strengths, or jobs that help you improve in areas where you are weak? Do you need to be good at everything? Should you avoid jobs where your weaknesses might materially undermine your performance?

This process takes hard work. It requires several steps. It also requires that you have a high level of motivation to be more self-aware and to face reality. It rests on a deep desire to improve. As noted earlier, you won't be able to do this all by yourself; you will need to seek the advice and observations of others. Each of us has blind spots that are painfully apparent to others. As a result, our own assessments take us only so far. Others observe us and can provide a reality check—but only if we ask.

Why Do We Fail to Understand Our Strengths and Weaknesses?

Much has been written about the importance of understanding our strengths and weaknesses.[1] Books, classes, and seminars focus on improving the capacity of professionals to do their jobs. Business leaders regularly speak about the importance of talent development. Most companies put an enormous effort into various types of training as well as annual reviews and feedback processes designed to help employees develop their proficiencies.

Given all this investment and emphasis, you might assume that this ground is well covered. Yet when I speak with people who are trying to build their careers, they often struggle to describe their strengths and weaknesses—particularly the weaknesses. Why the difficulty?

Amid the day-to-day distractions and chaos of their jobs, it is easy for people to fail to take the time to accurately assess their skills. This neglect may feel fine in the short run, but it almost certainly catches up with them in the long run.

Most people simply haven't done a sufficient amount of focused work on this topic. As a result, they lack self-awareness. Additionally, they usually haven't cultivated coaches who could help them identify their skill deficiencies. In some cases, when they do get constructive feedback, they aren't sufficiently prepared to acknowledge or understand it. As a result, they never fully decipher what the feedback actually means, how to benefit from it, or how to act on it.

Consequently, a surprising number of thoughtful people cannot identify where they need to improve or cannot formulate an action plan to address skill deficiencies. Essentially, they're flying blind.[2]

Taking Ownership of Assessing Your Skills

A young product manager at a large consumer goods company was feeling frustrated and uncertain about his job. He expressed annoyance with his direct boss and believed he wasn't getting a fair shake at work.

After listening to his story, I asked him to describe his strengths and weaknesses. He paused briefly and then responded, "I think I am very good analytically. I think I'm a good conceptual thinker. I am very dependable and hard working."

"What about the weaknesses?"

He thought for a few minutes and then asked if I could elaborate.

"Sure," I said. "For example, what criticisms have you heard from your boss or other work colleagues?"

"None, really," he said. "They tell me to just keep doing what I've been doing."

I asked if he received the maximum eligible compensation in the previous year. "Actually, no," he said.

"So how did your boss explain that?"

"He didn't really explain."

I asked him again whether he was sure that no specific skill deficiencies had come up in his review. He shrugged and said that he honestly couldn't think of specific weaknesses his boss ever mentioned.

Then after a pause, he said, "Well, I can be very impatient. And maybe other people are more creative than I am? I really don't know." These were the rough beginnings of a stab at articulating his weaknesses.

We then discussed his mind-set. Did he really want to take ownership of the challenge of understanding his strengths and weaknesses, or did he think this was someone else's job?

He admitted that he hadn't really thought about it in those terms. He thought this was his supervisor's responsibility, and, more broadly, his company's. "After all," he said, "they know me and what they need from me."

We began to discuss the possibility that the frustration and anxiety he was feeling were really not the fault of his boss or the company. I suggested it would be hard to get to the root causes of his frustration unless he took greater responsibility for assessing his skill set. I explained that the state of his capabilities had a direct impact on his ability to meet the demands of his job and the expectations of his boss.

He acknowledged that he had never taken proactive action to assess his own skills. It felt uncomfortable to him. We discussed whether his concern about his job was deep enough to motivate him to stop, reflect, and take proactive steps that might be a bit awkward at first. He noted that several of his peers were taking these steps, and it was helping them move forward in their careers. He further realized that he needed to push himself to reconsider his entire mind-set and approach to this vital area.

This story may seem like an exaggeration. On the contrary, it's typical. Most of us can't accurately write down our strengths and weaknesses. Maybe we could have at one point, but then the demands of our job changed, or we got promoted into a challenging new role and failed to update our thinking. Meanwhile, we began to feel silly, or even uncomfortable, continuing to solicit advice about identifying and overcoming our weaknesses. We may have believed our company was supposed to take the lead on this. After all, with all the review and coaching processes in place, is there really a need to do anything more?

At Goldman Sachs, I urged each professional to go well beyond formal processes. I encouraged employees to make it their mission to write down their strengths and weaknesses and then seek advice about techniques for addressing key issues.

Unfortunately, somewhere along the line, many professionals stop thinking proactively about skills and deficiencies. We're all human, and there are usually more enjoyable things to think about.

Letting this challenge slide is a serious mistake.

The First Step: It's About Specific Skills

Much of the confusion regarding capability assessment arises from the fact that the discussion tends to get mixed in with lots of non-skill-related topics. Well-intended coaches sometimes talk in vague and amorphous language about personal characteristics, politics, and general impressions, rather than deal with their observations regarding specific skills. As a result, the intended recipient is often left confused and unsure of what to do next.

The Power of Specific and Actionable Feedback

A young manager came to me for advice about feedback she had just gotten in her review. The primary guidance she had received from her supervisor was that she needed to "raise her profile." She described leaving the session feeling confused.

I, too, didn't understand her supervisor's comments. I had worked with her previously, and during those interactions, I had observed specific skills I thought she needed to improve. For example, I believed she could improve her presentation skills, and I recommended certain exercises and training that might help. I also felt she needed to improve her organization and time management skills.

I wondered why she hadn't gotten this kind of feedback from her direct boss, who presumably knew her far better than I did. How could he have conducted her performance review without getting into these kinds of issues? Maybe he had failed to do enough homework to home in on the skills she needed to address. Maybe he didn't associate coaching with addressing specific skills. Was it possible he wasn't a very effective coach or was simply inexperienced?

These are common problems. Often, even the most well-intentioned senior managers convey little more than their impressions, which are not grounded in hard observation or linked to specific capabilities. This puts the onus on the recipient to ask questions and generally to be proactive in trying to understand.

As the would-be beneficiary of constructive feedback, you often have to take steps to focus your coach or reviewer on specifics. You need these specifics in order to understand your skill deficiencies so that you can take constructive actions to improve.

Here are examples of steps you could take to be more proactive before, during, and after a review or coaching session:

- Before the session, write down your own assessment of your skill-based strengths and weaknesses. This will give you context for asking questions.

- Don't be bashful about asking questions during the session. This is different from debating or disagreeing. Your focus should be on understanding. Potential questions could be as simple as, "Could you explain that a bit further? Could you be more specific? What skills should I work on to address this? What specific actions would you advise me to take?"

- Be aware that a year-end review is rarely the best forum for getting coaching. Reviewers have numerous reviews to accomplish in a short period of time, and they may be as nervous as the people they are reviewing. If you're confused by some of the feedback and if simple questions do not clarify, suggest a follow-up session where you and the reviewer have more time to discuss the feedback and criticism.

- Recognize the possibility that your current boss is not going to be your best coach (and may not even be a good coach). You may go through periods when you have a boss who is not skilled at giving you constructive feedback. As a result, you need to proactively seek out the feedback of others who observe you, even though they may not have a reporting relationship to you. Those sources of coaching can be invaluable. Ask them probing questions about your strengths and weaknesses—and be prepared to do the same for them if they request your feedback.

The effort to assess skills is not about politics, connections, and popularity. It must be kept separate from attributes like good looks and other personal characteristics you can't easily alter. It's not about "good" and "bad." Rather, it's about facing reality and getting into clear specifics regarding skills. With that understanding in hand, you can then focus on the actions you need to take. This approach will require you to develop a game plan that might involve tailored exercises, job experiences, or training. Alternatively, it might impact your decisions regarding team selection, work environment, and job assignments. Finally, after a reasonable period, you will probably want to circle back with your boss or coach and assess the progress you've made.

Create a Skills Checklist

In doing this work, it helps to start with a common language. In particular, what do I mean by the term "skills"? Here are some examples:

Written communication

Speaking/presentation skills

Interpersonal skills

Listening skills

Analytical skills (not necessarily quantitative)

Organizational skills, including the ability to set priorities

Ability to delegate

Sales skills

Relationship-development abilities

Negotiating skills

Ability to confront others constructively

Coaching skills

Mathematical and quantitative skills

Conceptual skills (ability to see the big picture)

Physical abilities (if relevant to the job)

Second language skills

Specific technical knowledge and domain expertise (including technical areas such as accounting, technology, etc.)

Too often, people spend a great deal of time on feedback sessions without clearly addressing these specific abilities. Why? In many cases, the person giving the feedback doesn't connect his or her comments with skill development, and the recipient fails to ask about specific skills. Neither party has a skills mind-set in the session.

"Won't" Versus "Can't"

A businessperson recently asked me for advice regarding how to figure out his weaknesses. He seemed determined to demonstrate that he was thoughtful, self-aware, and willing to be self-critical. He volunteered that there were things he just wouldn't do. For example, he said, "I don't like to pick up my clothes at home, and I refuse to keep a clean desk at the office."

I asked him if he believed he was disorganized.

"Oh, no," he said quickly. "No, I'm not *disorganized*. I just don't like to pick up my clothes or worry too much about a clean office."

I responded that, even though this was an interesting observation, it didn't seem to be skill based. He was describing a choice rather than a capability. I then asked him to refocus on a capabilities list, as described in this chapter. When he did so, he said he wasn't sure he had any weaknesses.

Of course, this couldn't be true. The real problem was that he hadn't thought about his weaknesses *as* weaknesses. It was far easier for him to discuss things he "hated to do" than to admit there were certain fundamental skills he struggled with, because admitting that would mean he wasn't as great as he hoped—in other words, that he actually had weaknesses. I told him I was pretty certain he was weak in at least one or two skill categories, and he should try again, this time using a skill list as a template.

Assessments of strengths and weaknesses must focus on your capabilities. It sounds so obvious, yet many folks choose to dance around this. Your bosses don't want to confront you because they don't want to upset you or because they haven't done enough preparation to be specific. You may not want to hear it, because you're human, and hearing about your faults doesn't feel good. So it's easier to discuss generalities. Although it may feel more pleasant, and safer, it won't help you identify key issues and ultimately improve.

Let's try a concrete exercise. Refer to the list of skills presented earlier. It is not intended to be all inclusive; rather, it will help you get started. Using this menu, rate yourself on each skill using a scale of 1 to 10 (with 10 being world class). Alternatively, set up three columns—plus, minus, and "not sure"—and put each of the skills into one of these columns.

The Prism: Your Skills Relative to a Job or Task

Now take this analysis one step further. How do your capabilities measure up compared to the needs of a specific task or job? Strengths and weaknesses are not absolutes. They are qualitative assessments of your skills relative to something else. In the standardized testing world, they are relative to those of a peer group. In a job, they are relative to the task requirements of a job.

For example, by most standards, I'm a fast runner (a strength). However, if you asked me to run the 100-meter dash in the Olympics, I would be considered slow (a weakness). Versus my high school peers, I was a 10; in the world-class context, find me a seat in the stands because I would be a 1 or a 2.

To take the analysis of your strengths and weaknesses a step further, you need to have a job or task in mind—either your current job or a prospective job. Implicit in this analysis is the existence of a peer group that does this job at a high level of proficiency.

I am approached regularly by students who are considering a range of job offers. Before getting to their own characteristics and capabilities, I first ask what specific tasks are most critical to each job. Very few people can give me a good answer. I point out to them that the key tasks essential to high performance in each of the jobs are likely to vary dramatically. Given the wide disparity in required skills, how realistic is it to think one person could be great at all of them?

In most cases, students realize that even though they have been to numerous company presentations and have even met with employees at various levels, they have not focused specifically on the question of key skills. More often, they've assessed the likability of the individuals they've met and have explored whether the company environment felt consistent with their values and aspirations. These criteria are important, but this kind of review doesn't take the place of a critical analysis of the tasks essential for success in that job.

You must ask these important questions. What makes a great "XYZ professional"? What distinguishes the person at this company (or in this department) who is doing a good job from the person who's doing a great job? What are the key tasks I must do well? Based on those tasks, what are the most important skills I need if I am to succeed here?

Needs Change Over Time

In doing this analysis, it is important for you to recognize that the answers to these questions are likely to change over time. For example, being a banker (my former career) requires excellent quantitative and analytical skills in the early career stages. In addition, you need to have (or quickly build) domain expertise about the markets and specific industries. It helps to have the ability to research, write, and communicate effectively.

As you become more senior, interpersonal and communication skills become more important. At that point, conceptual skills also become more critical. Can you put yourself in the shoes of the CEO, and—surveying all the facts and analyses—develop an overall judgment about what action makes the most sense for the company? You don't have to be great at all these things on Day 1, but you must believe that, with hard work and experience, you have the potential ultimately to excel in at least some of the key skills of the job.

It is never too late or too early to ask these questions. As the world and industries change, the requirements of jobs change. In addition, as you become more senior, the necessary skills will change. For all these reasons, your skills assessment must be a dynamic exercise that is updated regularly.

Take Responsibility for Doing This Exercise—Now

When do you need to start doing this assignment? My answer is, "Now." If you're a talented young person just embarking on your career, most companies will help you determine the specific requirements and skills of a given job. However, they will also expect you to have done the hard work of assessing your own capabilities relative to the demands of a particular job at the firm.

As you advance in your career, your company will assume that you are updating this analysis as your job changes, skills requirements change, and the industry changes. As you progress, you will likely need to work harder to seek coaching and get advice from those who closely observe you. Because of the challenge of doing the job, managing people, solving client issues, and navigating the general chaos of work, many of us let our skills focus lapse at some point in our career progression.

All of us can bring to mind someone who got off to a great start in his or her professional career, and then—for some strange reason—seemed to fizzle out. In my experience, this generally happens either because the person never got in the habit of doing this analysis, or because the person failed to update this work and adapt to the needs of the job as it evolved. A failure to get into the habit of thinking deeply about the capabilities needed in a particular job will eventually catch up with you. This effort requires ongoing introspection and analysis, and it gives you a target to shoot at as you develop your skills.

Do You Have to Be Great at Everything?

The sales manager for a Midwestern software company wanted to improve his capabilities so that he could excel in his job and go further in his company. He was forty years old. He had been with the company since its founding—he was one of the eight original employees—and he had moved up the ladder as the company grew to $250 million in annual sales and more than 750 employees. His current position was head of global sales, a department of approximately 45 sales professionals. While he was attending an executive training course at Harvard Business School, he came to see me about his career aspirations.

He described himself as energetic and a voracious reader of industry publications and web-based information. Even so, he wondered aloud if he was doing enough to "keep up with the industry and the evolution of our customers."

I asked him to name the top three skills required to excel in his job. First, he mentioned customer-relationship skills and product expertise. He then explained that management skills were becoming an increasingly important part of his job. In particular, he said, a superb sales manager had to be highly proficient at customer targeting, hiring key talent, articulating clear priorities, coaching, and delegating.

I asked him to rank himself on a scale of 1 to 10 along each of these dimensions. He ranked himself highly on the first skills—8's and 9's—but gave himself only 5's on hiring talent, setting priorities, coaching, and delegating.

Given this ranking, I asked him if he had developed a plan to address his deficiencies.

He confessed that he hadn't really thought about it. He just knew he needed to improve, which was the main reason he was attending a Harvard Business School executive education program. He asked if he really had to rank 8 or 9 on all these skills. Wasn't it enough that he was a superb salesperson who was an expert on the product offering, even if he wasn't as strong in managing others? In particular, couldn't he simply decide to spend more time out with customers and elevate one of his talented subordinates to the role of chief operating officer? The COO could take the lead in hiring and addressing day-to-day management tasks while he focused on overall strategy, building client relationships, and coaching salespeople in the field during his client visits.

This was a reasonable approach to getting the job done. He didn't need to be a 10 on every skill, but he did need to work with his team to be a 10 in the job.

As I've said, one of your key objectives should be to become more aware of your strengths and weaknesses. Then you can decide whether you should work on addressing your weaknesses or building on your strengths while delegating certain tasks to individuals who have a greater aptitude in your areas of weakness. You need to take steps that will improve your overall effectiveness rather than try to be great at every skill yourself.

Ultimately, the sales manager decided to take a combination of actions. He delegated certain key tasks to a newly created COO position and also sought out coaching to help improve certain of his key management skills.

You Need Coaching to Do This

Coaching is often misunderstood. To develop a realistic baseline assessment of your capabilities, you need to reach out to people who can observe you and are willing to tell you things you may not want to hear. Finding these people is tough. No one wants to unnecessarily offend you. To encourage others to give you candid advice, you need to show them you're sincere and impress upon them that you want and need their help.

At this point, let's draw a sharp distinction between coaching and mentoring. I have listened to many people over the years who tell me they are getting great coaching from outside mentors. These advisers have never set foot in their organization nor closely observed them day-to-day. Many of these same people report back to me after they receive their annual review from their boss or board of directors. They are mystified as to why the review pointed to deficiencies that their outside mentor never mentioned or doesn't agree with. They are inclined to think that there must be something wrong with the review process at their organization, and they resent the reviewers who are raising these issues.

Their confusion lies in the dramatic difference between mentoring and coaching. Although these two activities tend to be discussed as if they were interchangeable, they are not at all the same thing.

Mentoring is a particular kind of interaction. It involves the mentee telling the mentor a story and getting advice from the mentor in reaction to that story. The problem is that the mentor's advice is only as good as the story. Unfortunately, each of us has blind spots that impact the quality of the story we might tell an outsider. As a result, mentoring often misses major weaknesses that relate to significant blind spots of the person being mentored.

Coaching, in contrast, requires direct observation on some regular basis. The coach observes the individual in action and, based on that observation, identifies specific skill deficiencies and other behaviors that may need attention.

In some organizations, senior people regularly coach junior folks, whether or not the junior folks solicit it. In many other organizations, though, a senior person does this only in response to a request for coaching. As a result, unless specifically asked, the senior person might wait until the year-end review to highlight skill deficiencies. This is why many people profess to be shocked by criticisms they hear in their year-end review.

You may be lucky enough to have a coach or coaches who observe you, are insightful, and care enough about you to explain their insights in a manner you can understand. In my experience, you usually need to solicit this type of coaching, because many senior managers may prefer not to risk offending you if they can avoid it.

A good coach also gives you one or two specific suggestions for ways you can improve a particular skill. To do this, your coach needs to know your job well enough to offer good advice and needs to have thought about it sufficiently to make the advice specific and actionable.

Finally, a good coach is willing and able to follow up. He or she is open to hearing how it's going and offers follow-up suggestions that help you move forward.

This notion of coaching helps explain why many people don't get great advice from board members, strangers, or outsiders. As noted, outsiders don't observe you regularly. They can only respond to a narrative you create, one that may reflect significant blind spots.

One other variation on the coaching process involves getting a professional outside coach. I have used this technique several times, and it can be helpful, especially when inside coaches have tried but still can't seem to break through to the person. The outside coach comes in and interviews people who work directly with the subject. The coach then relays that information (usually without attribution) to the subject and makes suggestions on how the subject can address the issues.

This approach works best when it's used exclusively for developmental, rather than evaluative, purposes so that the recipient doesn't feel he or she is being judged. It shouldn't be your first choice, but it is worth trying if needed. I have seen it help talented professionals gain greater self-awareness, become more open to constructive criticism, and get over the hump of realizing they need to improve and figure out how they might get there.

Why Is There So Little Coaching?

Most people I talk with, either in groups or individually, say they don't have a coach at work. Yet in their athletic pursuits, they readily admit to actively seeking out and getting the benefit of great coaching. They don't make the connection that it is just as important to seek out a coach at work as it is in playing a sport.

The degree of coaching can evolve over time. Newly hired individuals typically tell me they're getting competent coaching. By the time people are a few years into their careers, however, they increasingly feel they are no longer being coached. The more senior the executive, the less likely he or she is to say that they have a coach. It is no wonder that promising younger professionals often go off track as their careers develop.

This is perplexing. With all the time and money being spent on coaching and review processes, how is it possible? Is all this effort devoted to developing people a big bust?

The key to getting the benefit of great coaching is *you*. Do you really want coaching? Are you willing to seek coaching actively, or do you passively wait for it to come to you? When you receive it, do you listen or do you feel compelled to explain why the coach is wrong? Do you wind up disliking or blaming the coach? Do you really want to be critiqued? Do you say you want coaching but send a clear vibe that you don't want to hear constructive feedback?

As noted, some new hires feel that they get good coaching support during their early days in a job. Then what happens in the following months and years? We change jobs or get promoted. New people are observing us, and we fail to develop new relationships that would give us the valuable coaching we need.

Whatever the case, this effort must start with you. Your mind-set must be that getting coaching is your responsibility. You will be amazed at the number of people who will try to help you if you are willing to ask. People respect and want to help those who are trying to help themselves.

Subordinates Can Help You Figure It Out

The new chief executive of a nonprofit organization was frustrated. This organization helped disadvantaged kids through a variety of mentoring, after-school, and summer tutoring programs. The organization was well funded and had a good reputation. The founder had left to work in the government, but most of the original board remained in place. The new CEO had been the founder's chief lieutenant for many years.

Historically, her annual reviews with the CEO and board had always been superb. In her first review after one year in the job as CEO, however, it was a different story. The board raised several concerns regarding her organizational skills, suggesting that she was doing too much herself and not putting enough energy into coaching her direct reports. In her eight years with the organization, this was the first time she had ever received these kinds of criticisms. Although the board was supportive and encouraging, she left the evaluation session unsure about the criticisms. She didn't know how to interpret them and why this was happening now.

She came to visit my office and asked, "What changed?"

When I posed the question back to her, she wondered aloud if the board members simply missed the previous CEO. Maybe she hadn't done a good enough job cultivating relationships with them—which, of course, had never been her job previously. She wasn't sure she was going to enjoy this new role. She even asked me about alternative career options she might pursue in the event she decided to quit.

I suggested she write down the three most important tasks necessary for excelling in her previous job. Then I asked her to do the same exercise for her current job. How were they different? How would she rate her capabilities in the new job?

It turns out that the previous CEO had done most of the coaching of the nonprofit's employees. He had set the vision, communicated it, and coached people with the vision in mind. In her former role, the new CEO had relied on that resource and mainly had executed the directives articulated by her boss. In fact, as she was beginning to realize, she had also served as the informal coach of the previous CEO, providing useful feedback and a reality check when needed. In her new role, she was now the one who had to set the vision, communicate it, and coach people. She hadn't fully realized this, and she had no real experience doing it. Accordingly, she needed help and advice.

I encouraged her to identify one or two subordinates in whom she had confidence and from whom she could seek advice. She had never followed this practice with her own subordinates, even though her predecessor had done this with her.

A few months later, she reported that she now understood why the board gave her the feedback they did. They were, in fact, trying to help her. After the board's review, she had begun to actively solicit advice and feedback from key subordinates, and it had proven enormously helpful. She realized that for the first time in years, she was improving and developing new skills. "I think I'm going to be pretty good in this new job," she said. "I realize that I *do* like it. I just had to make a few adjustments and learn how to go about it."

Do you seek coaching from subordinates as you become a more senior person? No matter what your industry or function, this is vital to your success: assessing the key requirements of the job, assessing your own capabilities, and developing approaches to address your deficiencies.

What to Do About a Skills Mismatch

Should you consider changing jobs?

The story you've just read is typical of folks who have been promoted into a bigger job and find they're uncomfortable in the new position. There are many reasons a skills mismatch may arise. Maybe the person chose the wrong job. Maybe, like the new CEO at the nonprofit, he or she got a promotion. Maybe the world changed, and the demands of the job changed. Maybe the person's strengths were so compelling that key people around them compensated for their weaknesses—until the day one of those key people left, and the weaknesses began to impede their performance.

For you, the first step is to assess the match. If there's a mismatch, you need to pin down the reasons and take constructive action.

Maybe Your Boss Can Help

A young manufacturing supervisor at an industrial goods company started to believe that he was not a good fit for his job. This wasn't a superficial judgment; he had done his homework. He had worked diligently on assessing his strengths and weaknesses. He had sought advice from his direct boss as well as from colleagues and subordinates in his work unit. He did a reality check with several people who knew him from outside the workplace but had insights into his skill set. He thought deeply about the critical needs of his job.

What did he learn? He concluded that the person in his seat needed to be analytical, good at managing people, and able to focus on process improvements and understanding processes generally. "But the truth is," he told me, "I'm not great at the process-improvement part of this job. I'm a pretty good manager of people, but this is not a particularly strong or distinctive skill for me. I do well writing, communicating, and selling. I also seem to work better with people who are outside the company. I think I am better at building relationships with customers than I am at navigating a factory floor."

All this had led him to wonder if he should start looking for new opportunities outside the company. He didn't want to settle on this conclusion because he admired the company, liked the atmosphere, and took pride in the fact that it manufactured a product.

I asked him if there wasn't a viable solution that would allow him to stay at the company. Wasn't it possible that his bosses might well appreciate his thoughtful self-assessment and be highly motivated to find a way to keep him?

He decided to have a serious talk with his boss. His boss respected his initiative in raising these issues and encouraged him to set up meetings with several other senior people in the company. In each meeting, he described his strengths and weaknesses as well as his desire to find a way to continue moving forward in the organization. Several of the senior people suggested that he might be a great fit for the sales function. The timing was fortuitous because the company was working to upgrade the quality of this effort as a vital strategic priority.

As a result of these discussions, he moved from the manufacturing role to a role in the sales force. It turned out to be a great fit, and he hit the ground running. He reported a year later that he had already been promoted to a bigger role, and he appeared likely to go much further with the company in this role than he would have in his previous function.

This career move wouldn't have been easy to visualize in advance. It became possible only because this person really did the work to learn about his skills and then match them to key tasks in his current job and, later, against prospective jobs. He also took the big step of reaching out for advice and coaching. His terrific advance work created a clear basis to change departments and helped him unleash his greater potential and move his career forward.

Many folks are in the right company or industry but not the right function. For others, the right match between job and skills may require going to another company or industry. Whatever the case, doing the analysis and being self-aware will make it easier to envision this move and certainly more practical to accomplish it.

You Don't Have to Be Good at Everything

It bears repeating: you don't have to be good at everything.

I have worked with many professionals who have one or two strengths and a number of weaknesses vis-à-vis the job they're in. This doesn't necessarily mean they need to move.

For example, a junior person working in a financial services firm was uncertain whether to stay with her company. She had excellent analytical talents, market knowledge, and client skills. On the other hand, quantitative skills were not her forte, and she struggled when it came to doing financial modeling. Some of her peers suggested that if she wasn't good quantitatively, she probably couldn't compete effectively and be outstanding in this job. They suggested she consider getting out of the part of the business that involved stock-picking and company assessments and instead go into sales.

She went to a couple of senior folks in her unit to solicit their advice. They observed that although her quantitative skills were only adequate, she was so good at her other strengths that she might be able to offset her weaknesses by teaming with others on her client teams. A few of the senior folks even confided that they themselves hadn't been great at financial modeling, but this weakness hadn't prevented them from being successful. As a result of this advice, she decided to stay in her current job.

As she moved up to more senior positions, she found that her job required less modeling, although she did have to become proficient at reviewing the quantitative work of others. She learned that she had sufficient skills to coach subordinates on how to complete the quantitative work, and she was able to draw on her other skills much more heavily. She also learned that she wasn't expected to do this job by herself and could surround herself with colleagues who helped her compensate for her weaknesses. She ultimately emerged as one of the top professionals in her unit and at her firm. This is a lesson I learned in my own career: the capabilities of my assembled team needed to fit with my own skills and skill deficiencies.

Develop Critical Skills via Community Volunteer Work

I regularly ask young people who solicit my advice if they're involved in nonprofit and community activities that let them contribute their services and talents. They often answer that they'd like to—maybe someday—but right now they just don't have the time. Others say that donating money is their primary way of giving back.

It's easy to underestimate the numerous benefits of doing work in the community. First, because you're talented and energetic, you'll help your community and have a positive impact. Second, you'll get out of your element and gain the chance to try out new skills in a different context. You will learn a lot about yourself and your capabilities while helping other people.

This work can take a variety of forms. I actively work with a nonprofit organization that helps disadvantaged kids. Each student in the program is coached by an adult, who gets to know that student very well. I have seen numerous young adults learn how to become more effective coaches in this setting. At our events, the young adult is usually asked to get up in front of a crowd and describe his or her relationship with the student. For many participants, this is the first time they've coached someone and the first time they've had to speak in front of an audience. They learn how to do it and often realize they can be good at it.

At the same time, they also get feedback from their students as well as from many of the full-time professionals who run the program. I have seen a number of people gain an understanding of themselves and their skills and become more confident in their capabilities by doing community activities like this one. This is wisdom that they take back to the workplace and put to good use as they rise in their careers.

You Must Own This

The core concept in this chapter can be stated simply: take ownership of understanding your skills.

Doing so is a mind-set. It gives you a road map for assessing your strengths and weaknesses. It requires you to be proactive and not wait for the year-end review. It encourages you to take the initiative in seeking the observations and advice of those who are best positioned to observe you.

Take another look at the questions at the beginning of this chapter, and see if you can develop a game plan for answering them. Have you changed your mind about your answers to some of them?

Keep in mind that most companies and bosses won't do this for you. If you take the lead, however, you will find that your company and other colleagues will actively help you. In particular, you've got to take the leap of thinking like an owner regarding your career and your capability development.

An additional way to learn is to help others develop their capabilities. Coaching and helping another person assess his or her capabilities can teach you a lot about how to assess your own. Take advantage of these opportunities. I assure you that you'll get more out of it than you give.

Finally, get into the habit of writing down your thoughts in this area. It is one thing to think about how you might answer the questions posed in this chapter, and quite another to take a stab at writing them down. Committing your thoughts to writing will help you crystallize your thinking and will raise new questions you need to pursue.

Assessing your strengths and weaknesses is an essential first step toward reaching your potential. It gives you the foundation for doing the work described in the following chapters.

Suggested Follow-Up Steps

- Once you've finished the skill assessment exercise described in this chapter, discuss that assessment with someone who observes you regularly in a professional or work setting.

- If you are struggling to cultivate coaches, identify two or three seniors, peers, or subordinates who could coach you. Schedule time to meet with each individually, and push yourself to solicit their feedback. What do you learn from these sessions?

- Write down the top three skills you need to develop if you are to be outstanding in your current job. How do your skills match up with those job demands?

- Be available to coach others whom you regularly observe. What do you learn about yourself and your capabilities from these interactions?

CHAPTER THREE

Finding Your Passions

Dream the Dream

- How do you identify your passions?
- What do passions have to do with high performance and material success?
- Why is it so hard to translate your passions into a productive career?

Have you ever noticed that highly effective people almost always say they love what they do? If you ask them about their good career fortune, they're likely to advise that you have to love what you do in order to perform at a high level of effectiveness. They will talk about the critical importance of having a long-term perspective and real passion in pursuing a career. Numerous studies of highly effective people point to a strong correlation between believing in the mission, enjoying the job, and performing at a high level.[1]

So why is it that people are often skeptical of the notion that passion and career should be integrally linked? Why do people often struggle to discern their passions and then connect those passions to a viable career path? When people hear the testimony of a seemingly happy and fulfilled person, they often say, "That's easy for them to say *now*. They've made it. It's not so easy to follow this advice when you're sitting where I'm sitting!" What they don't fully realize is that connecting their passions to their work was a big part of how these people eventually made it.

This challenge doesn't come up only at the start of your career. It keeps coming up again and again throughout your life. Typically, you will first confront this issue with your initial job decision, and you will continue to confront it regularly over the course of your career. At some point down the road, you may wonder if there was another path you could have followed. You may start to have deep regrets. You may wonder if it's too late to pursue your dreams.

At various stages of your career, you may have a nagging feeling that others seem to enjoy what they're doing more than you do. Maybe they're in their own business or doing something that isn't as lucrative as what you're doing—and yet they somehow seem a lot happier than you are. Is it true, or does the grass always seem greener on the other side of the fence?

I hear these stories and concerns every week. I sympathize because I have struggled—and still struggle—with these questions. I regularly speak with corporate executives who are reaching a crossroads in their careers—individuals who don't want to keep doing what they're doing and are trying to carve a path that will allow them to continue learning and help them feel fulfilled.

The Pursuit of Passion

The purpose of this chapter is not to tell you what you should think about these questions. Instead, it challenges you to be more self-aware and more open to thinking about your passions. The only judge of how you balance what you learn is *you*. This chapter is intended to help you refocus on the fact that this is about you, and not about others and their opinions. If you're using others and their perceived expectations of you—or using your current circumstances—to justify your actions, this chapter may cause you to ask whether you're using these as a crutch or an excuse. You are the driver of the decisions you have made and will make. You own what you do, for better or for worse.

I encourage you to think about how you can discern your passions. This chapter presents several exercises and mental models that may help you achieve improved self-awareness and create a better prism for assessing how much you enjoy your current job or might enjoy prospective jobs.

This chapter then reviews how to connect your passions with achieving success in your career. In particular, how should you factor in your passions with your job and career choices? Are there activities that you can pursue in addition to your day job that might give you a portfolio of activities that satisfies you?

I also discuss how you might want to think about your life looking back decades from now, and how that might influence your thinking today. Equally important, I talk about the question of money and material success and explore how it relates to following your passions.

The timing and phasing of these judgments most likely will require you to make a number of trade-off decisions and develop new mental models for thinking about your life. I don't advise you which models to choose. Instead, I focus on helping you make your choices more explicit. In particular, we will discuss the importance of being aware of the trade-off decisions you're making, rather than being pushed or pulled into them.

Finally, we'll consider the numerous impediments to doing this work and discuss how you might become more aware of these impediments and therefore address them effectively. I use the word "work" in describing this process because the effort to gain greater self-awareness is absolutely hard work. It is like getting ready to play a sport you love or getting in better physical condition. It requires you to use new muscles and strengthen other muscles that may have atrophied. Like a good athlete getting in shape, you may find that using these muscles is uncomfortable and even painful at first. However, it should be a lot more satisfying once you've gotten in the habit of doing this work.

Understanding Your Passions

The word "passion" is frequently used in connection with emotions and feelings. It's about excitement. It has more to do with your heart than your head.

Passion is critical because reaching your full potential requires a combination of your heart *and* your head. In my experience, your intellectual capability and skills will take you only so far.

Regardless of your talent, you will have rough days, months, and years. You may get stuck with a lousy boss. You may get discouraged and feel like giving up. What pulls you through these difficult periods? The answer is *your passion*: it is the essential rocket fuel that helps you overcome difficulties and work through dark times. Passion emanates from a belief in a cause or the enjoyment you feel from performing certain tasks. It helps you hang in there so that you can improve your skills, overcome adversity, and find meaning in your work and in your life.

Early Career Passions

I regularly ask my students to describe their passions. Many say they don't yet know what their passions are. Why? For one thing, they haven't held many jobs, and they aren't sure what day-to-day activities are involved in various potential jobs.

To get them rolling, I ask them to think about which academic class they love. Most can immediately think of a particular subject or two. This can be tricky, though, because students tend to associate what they love with what they're good at and dislike subjects with which they struggle. You tend to gravitate toward what you get positive reinforcement for doing, even if it is not your favorite activity. Young people can also be highly influenced to like what their parents or other role models like, or want them to like, as well as what their peers think is cool.

I try to get young people started in the right direction by using a combination of exercises and mental models. I know that, over their early career, they will have transformative experiences, and they will learn, grow, and change their minds. The key is to help them choose a job that is in the general neighborhood of what they enjoy and where they can learn. From there, they need to be sufficiently self-aware and confident to pay attention to what resonates with them. This approach generally necessitates learning to filter out some advice of people who don't take the time to fully understand them but still feel free to enthusiastically project onto them their own likes and dislikes.

Midcareer Passions

In talking to more experienced people, I often have to get them to mentally set aside their financial obligations, their role in the community, and the expectations of friends, family, and loved ones. It can be particularly difficult for midcareer professionals to understand their passions because, in many cases, the breakage cost of changing jobs or careers feels so huge to them that it's not even worth considering. As a result, they try not to think too deeply about whether they like what they're doing.

The problem for many midcareer people is that they're experiencing a plateau that is beginning to alarm them and diminish their career prospects. This plateau is often a byproduct of lack of passion for the job. It may be that the nature of the job has changed or the world has changed, and the mission and tasks of their career no longer arouse their passions. In other cases, nothing has changed except the people themselves. They simply want more meaning from their lives and professional careers.

Of course, these questions are never fully resolved. Why? It's because there are many variables in play, and we can't control all of them. The challenge is to be self-aware.

The Beloved Doctor's Career Dilemma

A good friend of mine is a prominent doctor in a Midwestern town. He is loved by his patients and well respected in the community. He went into medicine because he wanted to help patients and—yes—because he believed it was a prestigious and lucrative career.

After finishing his internship and residency, he started in private practice by joining a partnership with three older doctors. It worked well. They split up the weekend on-call duties, and my friend slowly built up a strong following of patients. He joined the local country club and became a proficient golfer. He was an active leader in his church. Over the years, the partnership recruited additional doctors, the older partners ultimately retired, and my friend became the group's senior partner.

During this same period, managed care became more predominant, malpractice insurance costs rose dramatically, and the administrative costs of running his office soared. His take-home pay was declining even though his work hours were increasing. He found that, as the senior partner, he had to spend more time giving direction to the office administrative staff and less time with patients. He began to get annoyed more frequently than before. Eventually, he began to daydream about quitting and doing something else.

A large pharmaceutical company approached him with a lucrative offer to join the firm to help market its products and give speeches around the country. It was an offer he would have spurned years earlier, but by now he was so tired of the hassles of running his own practice that he felt compelled to seriously consider it.

He visited me to discuss what he should do. He described how he now "hated" his job. I asked how that could be possible. He was great with patients, he had helped so many people, and he had a substantial amount of experience in treating disease and keeping his patients healthy. Most of all, he was still relatively young.

He said to me, "Hey, you're a businessman. You of all people should be sympathetic to me quitting and taking a job with more money and less bureaucracy."

I told him I wasn't so sure about that. "If you're leaving to do something you love, then I get it. Otherwise, I must admit, I *don't* get it. What do you love to do professionally?"

At this point, the conversation ground to a halt. In the midst of the chaos of doing his job, he realized, he hadn't actually asked himself that question in several years. He just knew that he hated the administrative burdens and bureaucracy.

He reflected for a few minutes on what he loved to do versus what he hated to do. "You know," he finally said, "I must tell you that I still love working with patients." In fact, he explained, he loved that more than anything else he could think of professionally. After talking further, he also realized that if he could no longer practice medicine, he would miss it terribly. Not surprisingly, it was easier for me to see this than it was for him because he had been so immersed in the aggravations of his job. We discussed whether there was a way to off-load some of his administrative duties and free himself to just see patients. Maybe this meant changing his affiliation with a local hospital.

Maybe it meant joining another practice. He wasn't yet sure, but he knew it was worth looking for an answer before jumping to do something he didn't love as much as he loved practicing medicine.

Ultimately, he found a way to reorganize his partnership and delegate some of his administrative activities. He also learned to accept a certain amount of administrative work because it was worth the joy of helping patients. This was a trade-off he now made explicitly, and it was helped by his focus on better understanding his passions.

Exercises to Develop New Muscles

Most of our professional days are chaotic. In fact, life is chaotic, and, sadly, we can't usually predict the future. It feels as if there's no time to reflect. So how are you supposed to get perspective on these questions?

I suggest that you try several exercises. These exercises may help you increase your self-awareness and develop your abilities to better understand your passions. They also encourage you to pay closer attention to and be more aware of the tasks and subjects you truly find interesting and enjoyable.

Your Best Self

This exercise involves thinking back to a time when you were at your best. You were great! You did a superb job, and you really enjoyed it. You loved what you were doing while you were doing it, and you received substantial positive reinforcement.[2]

Remember the situation. Write down the details. What were you doing? What tasks were you performing? What were the key elements of the environment, the mission, and the nature of the impact you were making? Did you have a boss, or were you self-directed? Sketch out the complete picture. What did you love about it? What were the factors that made it enjoyable and helped you shine?

If you're like most people, it may take you some time to recall such a situation. It's not that you haven't had these experiences; rather, you have gotten out of the habit of thinking about a time when you were at your best and enjoying what you were doing.

After sketching out the situation, think about what you can learn from this recollection. What are your insights regarding the nature of your enjoyment, the critical environmental factors, the types of tasks you took pleasure in performing, and so on? What does this recollection tell you about what you might enjoy now? Write down your thoughts.

An Ambivalent Student's Initial Job Choice

During my second year of teaching at Harvard, one of my MBA students came to see me about his job search. It was a tough job environment, and the search wasn't going well. He was pursuing jobs very similar to those sought by his classmates and was getting beaten out for these jobs by his peers.

I asked him to describe what he loved about the jobs he was seeking. He explained that it wasn't that he was so passionate about these jobs; instead, he had decided to pursue what his classmates believed were the best jobs.

I asked him if he believed he would enjoy the key tasks of these jobs. Did he have a passion for the mission in each of these professions? To each of these questions, he glumly gave me an ambivalent response. I suggested that the interviewers were picking up the same ambivalence I was observing. Then I asked him, "Why are you in my office?"

"Well, I just thought it made sense to come and tell you about my search, and see if you had any advice."

I said, "Could I ask you to think about what you might love to do?"

He paused and said he wasn't yet sure. Although he was twenty-nine, he wasn't yet certain he had enough experience to have developed a strong point of view on this topic.

I asked him to think of a situation in his life when he had been at his best. I urged him to take this question seriously and take a few minutes before responding. After a brief period, a big smile crossed his face.

I asked him, "Did you think of something?"

Yes, he had. He described the time he took over as the temporary head coach of a local junior high school football team. He did this part-time while he was working in his first job after college.

"Why was that such a great experience for you?"

He explained that the team had a losing record when he first became coach. He focused intently on getting to know each young man, worked to coach each on fundamentals, and rearranged some of the positions they played to better fit their skills. Equally important, he had succeeded in infusing them with confidence and focusing them on doing their best, rather than worrying so much about who won and who lost each game. He recounted how the team improved dramatically and finished the season with a winning record.

What could he learn from this experience that might help him think about his current job search?

"Well," he said, "I think I do love to coach people and manage. I really enjoy creating and working in a team-oriented environment. I like teaching. I think I would enjoy going to a company where I could learn to run a business unit. I think I would really enjoy managing people."

I asked which of the jobs he currently was pursuing would give him that opportunity. Was it a financial or money management job? No, probably not. Might it be a job at a consulting firm? In that context, he might learn to manage a small project team, but he probably wouldn't get the opportunity to run a sizable business unit. These first two types of jobs were likely to be more about building analytical and advisory skills than about coaching, leading, and managing business units or companies.

He concluded that he should revisit options that would allow him to do what he thought he might love.

Ultimately, after several weeks, he accepted an offer from an industrial company that had a leadership training program that would get him into a managerial role relatively quickly. In the job interview for that position, he later recollected, he was persuasive because his natural enthusiasm for the job came through loud and clear. Two years later, he reported to me that he was highly pleased with his job choice and was glad he hadn't pursued other options that might have impressed his peers but didn't really fit with what he truly loved. He was on his way.

This student's story struck me. It reminded me of the power of peer pressure. It also reminded me that most of us have to struggle to remember situations when we were at our best. I got a kick out of this story because it was the first time since I had known this student that I had seen him happy. I can't help laughing when I think about this seemingly dour young man, who lit up when he began talking about his passions. Imagine the impact of this passion on the people he works with! I have seen this situation over and over during my career: if you put people in jobs that they love, they will shine in ways that astound you.

Passion is the essential fuel that allows us to find a professional home, to hang in there, and to work through our weaknesses. It gives us a reason to keep fighting to get better.

The Power of Mental Models

Another approach to helping you think about your desires and passions is to use mental models. That is, assume *xyz*, and then tell me what you would do—and why. Here are examples of these models:

- If you had one year left to live, how would you spend it? What does that tell you about what you enjoy and what you have a passion for?

- If you had enough money to do whatever you wanted, what job or career would you pursue?

- If you knew you were going to be highly successful in your career, what job would you pursue today?

- What would you like to tell your children and grandchildren about what you accomplished in your career? How will you explain to them what career you chose?

- If you were a third party giving advice to yourself, what would you suggest regarding a career choice?

Although these mental models may seem a bit silly or whimsical, I urge you to take the time to try them, consider your answers, and write them down. You're likely to be surprised by what you learn. Each of them attempts to help you let go of fears, insecurities, and worries about the opinions of others—and focus on what you truly believe and desire.

Unfortunately, there are people who have had to answer the "limited time to live" question for real. I have gotten to know some of these individuals. How they handled their situations taught me about human potential and the enormous capacity we have to overcome adversity if we have a passion for a cause.

Three Sisters Looking for a Cure

Jenifer Estess was my friend. She was an aspiring theater producer who was diagnosed with ALS—also known as Lou Gehrig's disease—in 1997, at the age of thirty-five. She had an older sister, Valerie, who was a gifted writer, and also a younger sister, Meredith, who worked in a job that used her keen business and organization skills. The three sisters were very close.

Jenifer was single, and Valerie and Meredith were both married with children.

ALS strikes approximately five thousand new people in the United States each year. There are no effective treatments, and it is almost always fatal within three to five years of diagnosis.

When confronted with Jenifer's diagnosis, the three sisters intensively researched the disease and visited leading scientists and clinicians. They learned that there were no treatments and were advised to begin planning for Jenifer's death. Their reaction to this advice was to fight. Their passion was not only to help their sister but also to help other sufferers avoid the bleak prognosis they were facing. The sisters dreamed of a day when ALS patients would not have to face the hopelessness they had to endure.

Their passion drove them to create Project A.L.S. in 1997 and work full-time to raise money to fund groundbreaking medical research, create teamwork among researchers and clinicians, and work toward finding a treatment for ALS. They have made enormous progress and have been leaders in the field of ALS research. Their efforts have jump-started research and collaborations that hopefully will lead to finding a treatment for this dreaded disease.

Jenifer passed away in 2003, but the fight continues, driven by the passion of the Estess sisters and numerous others who have joined the cause. These three sisters had no science or medical background. In fact, they may have been among the most unlikely folks on the planet to make the enormous impact they have made. A major part of the explanation for that impact is their passion for the cause.

I hope this type of challenge and tragedy doesn't confront you. At the same time, I do hope you'll seriously consider the question of what you would do if something like this happened to you. Don't wait for a horrible diagnosis before you work to figure out how you would like to spend your time. In addition to spending precious time with family and friends, is there a cause or mission that arouses your passion? If so, why wait until you're confronted with a finite time limit? Why not pursue this passion now, with at least a portion of your time?

Try working through the mental models presented here. They may help you gain insight about what you love and what tasks you might enjoy. They will improve your awareness and have a positive influence on your decision making.

The Role of Trade-Offs and False Trade-Offs

Invariably, a discussion of this topic leads to the issue of trade-offs. Many people feel that there must be an inherent tension between following passions and pursuing a lucrative career. I have heard many students say they have plotted out a career course in which they'll focus on making money now and pursue their passions later.

The problem with this logic is that it fails to take into account the powerful impact of passion on career success and high performance. In addition, it fails to consider that once you head down a career path, it can be enormously difficult to radically shift course and dramatically change your career. It's one thing to make a change within an industry or company where the job is adjacent to what you've been doing. It is quite another to attempt to make a radical change in industry or job functions without first taking a dramatic step backward to retool and start over.

Money Versus Passion: A Flawed Trade-Off

In my experience—almost without exception—you need to have a sufficient level of passion for your current job in order to be at your best. Of course, there are likely to be elements of the job that you don't enjoy, but there must be enough activities that you *do* enjoy if you are to perform at a high level for an extended period. Unless you strike oil, financial benefits normally are *back-end loaded:* they tend to come after a sustained period of high performance. If you believe that one of your primary goals is money, you need to be prepared to consistently perform at your best for a number of years.

I encounter many people who fervently believe they want to maximize their money, status, power, and position. These motivators—sometimes referred to as *extrinsic* motivators—can't be ignored. At the same time, you can't make the fundamental mistake of ignoring *intrinsic* motivators. These include learning, passion for the cause, relationships, skill development, culture, a feeling of belonging, comradeship, and other intangibles.

Again, to be at your best for an extended period, you need to enjoy a certain number of intrinsic motivators in your job. This puts the onus on you to assess whether a sufficient number of these factors are in place early in your career.

In addition to the delay in fulfilling your extrinsic motivations, you need to be prepared for the possibility that some of them may never materialize because of broader trends such as commoditization of products, new industry developments, and global economic shifts. On the other hand, there's also the possibility that certain careers you haven't thought of as lucrative will turn out to have great material rewards if you are truly outstanding.

You must accept the fact that, no matter what the job, you're not likely to become rich or famous or leap to the top of a company during your first few years. In fact, it is often a long slog before you attain many extrinsic goals. This is true even in the most lucrative careers.

I emphasize these points because I am regularly visited by people who chose jobs that manifested many of the extrinsic goals they thought they desired. After a brief period, they began to realize they didn't actually enjoy the job sufficiently to work through the frustrations and challenges that are typical in the early stages of a career. The ultimate extrinsic motivators were great, but these prospective rewards didn't help them actually enjoy the day-to-day grind.

Stated more bluntly, they couldn't stand their jobs, and the promise of future money was not sufficient to get them to stay with it. They were shocked to find out that some amount of intrinsic motivation (enjoyment of the job tasks and belief in the mission) was necessary to pull them through the day-to-day challenges of doing the actual job.

No job is perfect, of course. But to cash in on the rewards you may seek, you must enjoy a job enough to stay with it. The more you enjoy the job, the more likely it is that you will have the motivation to address your weaknesses, seek coaching, and take ownership of making the needed improvements in your skills.

Why is it that some people just seem to work harder at getting better and developing themselves? Is it their natural work ethic? More often, I have found that their passion is what gives them the energy and motivation to apply the work ethic they need to excel. Do you have enough passion for what you do to sustain your work ethic? You need to ask, and answer, this question.

Why Should You Struggle with This?

These concepts seem simple enough. So why is it hard to do this work? You may be thinking about all the reasons you struggle to discern your passions and find the will to act on them. Maybe the exercises and discussions in this chapter have helped you, but you still aren't sure you can put these thoughts into action.

In my experience, there are a slew of reasons people struggle with these questions. As mentioned in chapter 1, two issues are the influence of peer pressure and the power of conventional wisdom. Peer pressure might include meeting the expectations of friends, family, and those in your circle. Conventional wisdom is the drumbeat of advice and messages we all receive as to what is hot, cool, valued, prized, desired, and appropriate. These messages are particularly powerful if you lack confidence and are insecure about what others think of you and who you are.

You will learn more in chapter 4 about your life story, traumas in your life, self-doubt, and the negative narratives in your head. You'll learn why these aspects of your life make it easier to do what others want you to do rather than rely on your own thoughts and instincts.

Another impediment is your assessment of your current circumstances. Very often, people appropriately say, "I would love to think about this, but I don't have that luxury; I am too pressed for money; I desperately need this job; I desperately need a job, *any* job; that 'unconventional path' ship sailed a long time ago; I am in this career for the duration; I'll think about what I want to do when I retire." As discussed in chapter 1, one of the rules of the road is that you must adjust to the reality of your situation. We all must live in the here and now and meet our obligations to family and loved ones. But the key is to make sure you're making this choice *explicitly*, based on your current situation. You want to be careful that you haven't adopted a mind-set that traps you in a vicious cycle, in which you stop considering what you enjoy because you start to find it easier to avoid making an explicit choice.

Do any of these objections ring a bell with you? They give you a reason not to bother exploring what you might truly enjoy. Some of them are understandable, but still, you must ask yourself why you're putting up with these objections. In considering these matters, I have found it useful to separate the *what* from the *how*. Figuring out *what* you're interested in has very little downside and a lot of upside. On the other hand, the question of *how* you deal with what you learn should be considered separately. Don't use uncertainty regarding the challenges of *how* as an excuse to avoid this work.

Other related objections include, "I don't want to let people down; I would love to change my life, but too many people are relying on me; they would freak out if I did something else; I can't do it right now; the economy is too weak, and this isn't the time for me to act on this." Very often, these objections are a substitute for, "I am scared. I fear the unknown. It could be a disaster. What if it doesn't work? I'm going to look like a fool."

Go one level deeper, and you may hear an inner voice saying, "I'm not good enough. I was never good enough. Everyone is going to know I'm not good enough. People who now think highly of me will no longer think highly of me. Those who love me might stop loving me."

OK, enough armchair psychology. I don't mean to dismiss or make light of these concerns. My goal here is not to suggest what you should or shouldn't do. Rather, the objective is for you to strive to be more self-aware. You must come to grips with what stands in the way of understanding yourself and your passions. Even if you choose not to act on this self-awareness, it will help you to better understand yourself. In particular, you'll improve your ability to make more explicit choices, weigh trade-offs, and gain a better understanding of why you're doing what you're doing.

Dream the Dream

Passion is critical in reaching your potential. Getting in touch with your passions may require you to give your fears and insecurities a rest and focus more on your hopes and dreams. You don't need to immediately decide what action to take or assess whether your dream is realistic. There is an element of brainstorming in this effort: you don't want to kill ideas before you've considered them. Again, allow yourself to focus on the *what* before you worry about the *how*. This exercise is about self-awareness, first and foremost. It is uncanny how much more likely you are to recognize opportunities if you're aware of what you're looking for.

This chapter suggests a number of ways to exercise some of your passion muscles. For many people, it will take practice, and it will be worth doing these exercises on a regular basis. If you manage other people, it is also worthwhile to encourage them to do the same. I can think of many occasions in my career when this effort has helped me keep colleagues from quitting, because we were able to reformulate their job responsibilities or find them another job at the company that better fit their passions.

Finally, it is often easier to help others do this work than it is to do it for yourself. Don't miss opportunities to help others figure out their passions. It will help you gain insight into yourself and improve your own ability to identify what you truly enjoy and make breakthroughs in your own career.

Suggested Follow-Up Steps

- Do the "best self" exercise described in this chapter. Make sure you write down the two or three insights you gained from this exercise.

- Try out at least two or three of the five mental models listed in this chapter. Write down your insights. Discuss these insights confidentially with another person.

- Based on these two steps, write down the tasks you enjoy. Without prejudging their merit, consider the other job aspects that you believe create enjoyment for you: mission, environment, other people, status, money, and so on. Do not attempt to edit out intrinsic versus extrinsic motivators.

- What stands in the way of you spending time on the activities you enjoy? Is there an action you could take that would remove one or more of these impediments?

CHAPTER FOUR

Understanding Yourself

The Power of Narrative

- What is your life story?
- What impact do your success and failure narratives have on your decision making and behavior?
- Do you understand why you behave as you do?

Once you have worked on assessing your skills and discerning your passions, you need to take an additional step before turning to strategies for developing your career and reaching your potential. This step involves coming to grips with your life story and understanding how it impacts who you are.

Understanding your own story might sound simple enough. Surely, you must be an expert on your own story. Or is it more complicated than that?

Every action you take gains meaning when it is viewed through the prism of who you are. The better you grasp who you are, the better you will be prepared to manage yourself and take actions that help you to reach your dreams.

Each person on this planet has a life story that is unique. Your story has a powerful impact on your emotions, perceptions, idiosyncrasies, assumptions, vulnerabilities, and mindset. Your story goes a long way toward explaining your behaviors.

It is often said that the most important person you'll have to learn to manage is *you*.[1] Understanding your life experience is critical to managing yourself and also to employing the techniques suggested in this book. You can't alter your life experience up to this point, but you can work to be more aware of how it impacts your behaviors—for better and for worse.

You need to write down your life story because it is a primary window into understanding yourself. This effort is about self-awareness. As the saying goes, you are the product of your past but the author of your future. Many people get tripped up as they attempt to author their future because they are unable to take constructive actions that would enhance their lives and careers—and they don't know why. Studying your past may help you understand why.

Many individuals describe situations in which they know the behaviors they want to avoid but still can't stop themselves from taking actions they know they'll regret. For example, they lose their temper in a tense business situation, even though they know it undermines their effectiveness and causes their peers to lose respect for them. Or they make a key decision in an unproductive manner and are not sure why. They fail to acknowledge a mistake on a minor matter because they fear that admitting the mistake will make them look stupid or incompetent. They can't bring themselves to disagree with a colleague on a business decision because they fear confrontation and debate. Sometimes they are consciously aware of what is driving them, and sometimes they are not.

Invariably, their life experiences can help explain what they're doing and why they're doing it.

I do not intend to play the role of psychoanalyst. I'm not qualified. Instead, this chapter will point out the powerful role of your life story in your efforts to reach your potential and encourage you to take steps to become more self-aware. This is a lifelong effort. Over time, it can pay massive dividends in helping you create the kind of career and life to which you aspire.

First Step: Write Down Your Basic Story

As a first step, write down the story of your life. I suggest you do this chronologically. Where were you born? Describe your parents, brothers and sisters, the town you lived in, the people you knew, and so forth. Try to recall specific and meaningful experiences during these years—incidents at school, key interactions involving your parents, and so forth. Carry this story right up to the present.

In this first pass, keep it very basic and descriptive. There's no need to overlay analysis and editorial comment on top of these events and facts (although you'll be tempted to).

For example, I was born and raised in Kansas City. My parents, Meyer and Florence, were born in New York City and moved to Kansas in 1951.

My dad was the youngest of eight children, and my mom had an older brother. My father's father died when my father was very young. My father grew up very poor in Brooklyn. As a youngster, I listened to my dad tell numerous stories about the struggles of his family. My mom's father was in the clothing business in New York City. He was a very aggressive stock market investor and was wiped out financially by the stock market crash of 1929. My parents met when they were sixteen and married when they were twenty. My father—who had enlisted in the army at the outset of World War II—shipped out to Europe right after the wedding. He spent the next three years fighting in Europe, and I grew up hearing about several of his harrowing wartime experiences. He returned home in 1946, went to work, and finished his college education in the evenings. In 1951, my father was offered the Midwest sales territory for a jewelry company, and my parents moved to Kansas.

I'll stop the narrative here, but you get the idea. I could fill several pages of recollections of their story, my story, and my experiences. Even as I write this, I am reminded of how strongly I was influenced by their life experiences.

The stories of their economic struggles growing up—and then our family's own economic struggles at various points—had a profound impact on my thinking, and it stays with me to this day. As a traveling salesman, my father drove fifty thousand miles a year to cover the stores he sold to across the Midwest. He was a commissioned salesman, so he only earned based on what he sold. My mom also worked. I remember how hard they worked. I remember their stories. I remember their advice. All this, as well as my own life experiences, have impacted who I am and have shaped the decisions I have made at every point in my life.

I must admit that until very recently, I never fully realized the powerful influence that my parents (as well as my own formative life experiences) have had on my behaviors. During my adult life, why have I often chosen to work all the time? Why have I always been relatively frugal with my personal spending and never particularly motivated by monetary rewards? Why have I always had a healthy skepticism regarding formal authority and conventional wisdom? Why did I choose to leave a lucrative career to teach at Harvard? Why was I often a perfectionist, sometimes feeling deathly afraid of not being at my best? Over all these years, was I even *aware* of these aspects of my behavior?

Like most people, I never took time to reflect on my life story and think about its implications. After a romantic relationship failed, an ex-girlfriend politely pointed out that my childhood experiences might be affecting me more than I realized. I had no idea what she meant, and I laughed it off. Occasionally, other people tried to open my eyes to some of my idiosyncrasies and even eccentricities. I admit that I didn't have a clue what they were talking about.

It wasn't until I began teaching with Bill George in a Harvard Business School class he created—"The Authentic Leader," based on his book *True North*—that I began to go back and think about all this.[2] (I more or less had to, because it was what we were asking our students to do.) I began to open my eyes to the powerful impact of a person's life story.

With my own story as a backdrop, let me again encourage you to take time to write your story in whatever form is easiest for you. It doesn't need to be perfectly written, and you don't need to show it to others. It's for you. The goal is to get the story down on paper. Take a stab at it. If your experience is like mine, this exercise will take a lot longer and be much more extensive than you may expect.

What Did You Learn?

After you're finished, take some time to reflect on your story. What did you learn?

You may be amazed by some of your observations and by the fact that you could be surprised by a story you thought you already knew. Maybe writing this story has caused you to realize that your parents (and upbringing) have been even more influential in your life's decisions than you thought. You may be surprised by the emotions you felt in recounting certain events. You may even start connecting a few dots—recognizing patterns in your own behavior and experiences that you haven't previously noticed.

Finally, you may begin to believe that you've never fully processed many of your life experiences and, as a result, are unsure how they impact your behaviors today. Whatever your reactions, writing your life story is an essential first step toward understanding your story and understanding yourself.

In my experience, this first step is a big one, and you may take a few weeks or more to write, reflect upon, and add to your story. The key is to get it written down.

You may start to refocus on specific events that you believe have been significant in impacting your behavior. As an additional step, you should take a stab at writing down how your overall story and specific events have impacted your behaviors, beliefs, and key decisions. Again, the question is—as it will be throughout this chapter—what can you learn? There's not a *good, bad, should*, or *shouldn't* in any of this. Instead, there's the question: what insights can you glean from all this?

Second Step: Understand Your Competing Narratives

After you've written down your story, it may occur to you that there are alternative narratives that would string together the threads of your story. In fact, you will probably realize that you have been telling others, as well as yourself, these various narratives for most of your life—in job interviews, when you meet new people, when you go on a date, when you talk to your children, and so forth. Let's take a look at possible narratives.[3]

The Success Narrative

Typically, the predominant narrative you tell others is your success narrative. This is a lovely story, usually with you playing the role of hero. If you're not sure what I mean, think of the stump speech or campaign advertisements of political candidates. They tell a story that puts them in a positive and empathetic light.

Take a stab at beginning to write down your success narrative.

Again, for illustration, here's a thumbnail sketch of my own success narrative. It takes the basic facts I recounted earlier and gives them a distinctly positive spin. I am a second-generation

US citizen. My parents were children of the Depression and World War II. They lived the American Dream, overcoming their modest backgrounds and becoming successful through hard work and dedication. They strived to succeed because they loved their family and wanted to give us better opportunities than they had.

I was inspired by their love and dedication. I wanted to be like them. I worked hard to make them proud and justify their sacrifices. Based on their inspiration, I have strived to succeed at school and in my professional career. I succeeded in business, and then I went to Harvard to teach in order to help others achieve success and reach their potential. My story is one of success and love, and it is a tribute to the American Dream. Anyone can succeed in this country with enough hard work and dedication.

This is a nice story. It's a *winning* story. Reading it might even bring a tear to your eye. It certainly makes my mother very proud. If my father were alive, it would make him very proud. This story would likely impress new people that I meet—if I told it to them.

There's just one issue: this is not the only narrative that is going on in my head or that knits together the facts of my story. Several other narratives grow out of the same set of facts and experiences.

The Failure Narrative

In particular, there's a failure (or self-doubt) narrative that could also be told based on the facts of my story. As you might guess, this is not such a glowing story. This narrative seldom gets told in a job interview or included in the "about the author" blurb on a book jacket. It is an alternative narrative that is present in my head.

If you met me or worked with me, you probably would have no idea that this narrative is in my head. Based on how I present myself to others, you might figure that all my thoughts about myself must be positive—even glowing. But it's not so.

Here's an example of the self-doubt narrative: my dad travelled and my mom worked. I was home alone much of the time. I loved my parents and have been deeply influenced by their challenging upbringing and their financial struggles. Their hardships caused me to worry quite a bit about them and made me feel that I needed to work extremely hard to justify all their sacrifices.

I was an anxious kid. I tended to sweat a lot, particularly in social situations. Have you ever seen the kid who perspires a lot at parties—especially when he's talking with girls? That was me. I was a bit awkward. In high school, I was a good athlete but an erratic student, mainly because I struggled to concentrate and lacked self-confidence.

When I moved away from home and went to college, I dealt with my awkwardness in a new way. I began to study—a lot. In fact, at college, I studied all the time. I was very anxious to prove something and do well. I then went to Harvard Business School, where I took a somewhat more balanced but similar approach.

I joined Goldman Sachs after business school. I loved the markets and the firm, and I felt right at home with all the other neurotic and highly achievement-oriented people at the company.

In one sense, the firm gave me a place to hide: I was always working and therefore didn't have to be very social.

I could go on, but this gives you the idea. The theme in this narrative is something along the lines of, "I'm not good enough" or "I don't fit in" or "My job is all I've got, so I'd better work my tail off."

Of course I exaggerate a little bit to demonstrate the point. Although I have grown, matured, and developed much more confidence in the ensuing years, the reality is that variations on this failure narrative are still sometimes in my head. Moreover, there are several other narratives that lie somewhere between the success and self-doubt narratives.

As you think about your own narratives, the key is not to try to control or block out these thoughts. The point is to be aware of them and try to understand them and, in particular, to try to understand how they impact your decisions and behaviors.

As I mentioned, people who work with me usually remark that they think I have all the confidence in the world. They would be surprised to hear that a self-doubt narrative could be in my head. This is because they see me from a distance and aren't intimately familiar with my life story. All they see is the résumé and a very confident person. On occasion, they may be taken aback by my intensity regarding a particular matter or how driven I am in general, but they don't know why I am acting this way.

Awareness of the Narrative in Your Head

The challenge for all of us is to be aware of these various narratives and try to understand how they may impact our behaviors.[4] When you have an important decision to make, which narrative is in your head? When you make a mistake or are under severe pressure, which narrative is in your head? When you do something you regret or just can't seem to allow yourself to do something you want to do, which narrative is in your head? How is that narrative impacting your decision making, perceptions, and behavior?

These are challenging questions because all of us struggle to figure out why we do what we do.

Third Step: Consider How Your Narratives Impact Your Behavior

Work on finishing the draft of your success narrative. Remember that, in this narrative, you are the hero. It may be the story your mom tells when she wants to brag about you to her friends. It may be the story you tell at a cocktail party. Give yourself permission to write down this story in all its glory.

Now move on to writing down your failure narrative. This will be tougher. It is probably a story that you don't tell very often—but it is alive and well in your head. This one is a story of self-doubt. It may be a narrative about not fitting in, being afraid you're not good enough, fearing failure, or failing to please others. It may be a story about feeling abandoned or fearing rejection. It may be a narrative in your head that you'd prefer not to write down. Maybe you'd prefer not to even acknowledge that you think it. But make the effort to write it down anyway. You will learn something from this exercise.

Once you've written these narratives, think about the circumstances under which each of them is in your head. Is it possible that, when you made a good or a confident decision, the success narrative was in your head? Conversely, has your failure narrative kept you from speaking up at work or asserting yourself in critical situations?

More generally, is the narrative in your head helping or hindering your ability to consider and act on what you truly believe in a given situation? Is the narrative in your head helping or hindering your ability to focus on what you love and to figure out what jobs excite your real passion? When you tell yourself that you can't do something, how is this conclusion influenced by the narrative in your head?

The Fear of Not Being Good Enough for My Father

A thirty-four-year-old sales manager for a media company located in the Northeast had worked in media sales since her graduation from college. Her father had been a serial entrepreneur, and her mother was an elementary schoolteacher. The sales manager made a good living and carefully saved a portion of her compensation every year. She was referred to me by a mutual friend, who asked if I could give her some advice.

When we met, she explained that she felt trapped. I asked her about her current job and the skill fit. It was clear to me that she was really terrific in her job and that it was an excellent match for her talents. The problem, as she explained, was that she just didn't have a passion for the product or the company's mission. As a salesperson, she wanted to feel enthusiasm for the cause.

I asked her why she hadn't quit. She explained that she didn't want to risk giving up her secure and stable income. As a result, she just kept plugging along.

When I asked her about her passion, she explained that she wanted to work on sustainability; she wanted to be involved in reducing greenhouse gas emissions and in improving the quality of food, air, and water. She had suffered from mercury poisoning as a teenager and felt strongly that part of her life should be dedicated to environmental causes. I asked if she could play this role on a volunteer basis rather than attempting to switch careers. That was the compromise she had made up to now, she replied, but she was beginning to feel dissatisfied with this arrangement.

After taking me through her situation, she shook her head and said, "This all sounds pretty stupid, doesn't it? With all the people out there who are looking for work, it must seem kind of silly for me to be so self-indulgent with this environmental interest. I should just suck it up and get back to work—and count my blessings. My career isn't the most important thing, anyhow."

I told her that I understood her point, but I wondered why she was talking herself out of pursuing her dream.

She thought for a bit and then said she had grown up in an economically challenged family. Her father loved to start businesses, and during her high school years the family always teetered on the edge of bankruptcy. As a result, her parents had scrimped and saved every penny. Her parents' struggles were always in her mind and caused her never to take money for granted.

I asked her to expand on this. "I'm not trying to push this too far, but I wonder if your parents' economic stress is unduly affecting your thinking on this."

With this encouragement, she explained that she was probably closer to her mother than her father. Her father always seemed preoccupied, and even somewhat bitter, while she was growing up, and she dealt with it by working hard to please him.

She explained that her father was still highly influential in her thinking. He often made it clear that he believed she should stay in her current job. Further, he didn't fully appreciate her sustainability passion. Even though he remembered her mercury-poisoning episode, he couldn't understand why that experience should have any impact on her career choices.

As she thought about it, she pinpointed the problem. It wasn't that she was afraid of making less money but that she was really afraid of letting down her father. To paraphrase, the narrative in her head was, "I don't think I'll live up to my father's expectations. Maybe I've let him down already!"

Her skills weren't holding her back. Her passions were clear to her. There were jobs out there in the sustainability field that she could pursue; in fact, her sales and marketing skills were attractive to a number of for-profit and not-for-profit environmental organizations. She wasn't afraid to make less money and cut back on her spending, but the expectations of her father—his story, her story, and the feeling of doubt in her head regarding his respect for her—acted as a dead weight around her neck.

Becoming more aware of this didn't change the way she felt or remove the narrative in her head. But it did make her more aware of why she was making the decisions she was making. This greater awareness, in turn, ultimately helped her decide to take a risk and change careers.

At last report, she is flourishing at an environmental non-profit. She is much more of a leader than she was in her previous job. She is building a reputation in the field. She is following her dream and is thrilled about her career. As it turns out, once she made the switch, her father was far more supportive and encouraging than she had expected. He is proud of what she's doing and is happy that *she* is happy.

It is amazing how often we thwart our own desires based on our fear of disapproval from others. Often, expressed disapproval comes from well-meaning friends and loved ones who want you to be happy and therefore caution you against choices that they believe will make you unhappy. Invariably, if you are happy, people who care about you will see that and will approve of the choices that led to your happiness. It takes most of us several rounds of trying to please others before we learn this lesson.

The Implications for You

What are the narratives swirling around in your head? Can you write them down? How do they impact your behavior? Are they helping you, or do they act as a ball and chain around your ankle?

This discussion is primarily about creating greater awareness. Everyone has a failure narrative—you, me, everyone. The challenge isn't about getting rid of it or morphing it into another type of thought. Instead, the challenge is to figure out how our narratives are impacting our behaviors—and, in particular, how and why they're holding us back. Is it justified, or only an old and unproductive relic of a previous phase of your life?

I urge you to try this analysis for yourself. You may think it's too touchy-feely—and maybe it is. However, it is reality. Part of reaching your potential is facing reality.

Another Variation on Your Story: Your Experience of an Injustice

There is an additional approach to understanding your story that I like to use. It relates to an injustice that you might have experienced. Maybe you got passed over for a promotion, you were rejected in a job interview, you didn't get paid what you thought you deserved, you got fired, you were misjudged or judged unfairly, or maybe you got a speeding ticket you thought was unfair.

I usually do this exercise with graduate students as well as executives. I first ask participants to think of an injustice that was done to them. I ask them to think of the specific situation and then write down the facts. What happened? What were the circumstances? What was their role in the injustice? How did they feel at the time?

In most cases, people initially struggle to recall such a situation. I encourage them to reflect for a few more minutes. Eventually, they think of something and start writing.

Typically, when I ask the participants to wrap it up, at least a few say they need more time and, in some cases, even appear to be angry. I ask them why, and they sheepishly explain that while at first they couldn't think of anything, they finally did think of a situation. "Now that I'm writing down what happened," they say in so many words, "I'm starting to get really angry. I can't believe I didn't think of it more quickly because it really upsets me now that I recall it."

I have seen this happen numerous times. Many of us can't easily think of a situation when we felt an injustice was done to us. Of course, if you've been fired without cause, you probably won't have a hard time recalling that situation. In most other cases, though, the recollection of an injustice tends to get submerged in our memories. Once we dredge it up, we realize that it's been there all along and that it might even have a substantial impact on how we think and behave.

Do the Injustice Exercise

Try to recall an injustice in your own life. Then ask yourself how you framed (i.e., developed a narrative to explain) this injustice at the time it happened—and then how you have since reframed it. Consider how this experience may be impacting your behaviors today. It might further help you to discuss this story with a trusted friend or colleague.

Most of us tend to initially frame an injustice one way and then later reframe it differently. For example, an executive might comment that he felt hurt and angry at the time he was fired ten or fifteen years earlier. He may further say he felt rejected—a failure.

That same executive might, today, frame the story very differently. He may even say that the firing was the best thing that ever happened to him. He may then go on to convey one or two pearls of wisdom he learned from the experience. Time, distance, and maturity have changed the way he views this trauma.

Of course, the moral of the story is not always so neat and tidy. The injustice may be having significant negative consequences for the person to this day—whether he knows it or not.

The Television Producer Experiences Injustice

A twenty-nine-year-old assistant television producer in the Southeast was feeling very frustrated and angry about his career. He previously had been passed over for promotion to full producer at his television station. He had searched for other producer jobs in the region, but he couldn't get anyone to take a chance on him. He described how the person who had gotten the job he coveted wasn't as smart or as skilled as he was.

"This is all a big political game," he told me, "and the people who get the jobs are the ones with the connections. All this talk about being a team player and helping others sounds nice, but it's not how people get ahead."

This is how he framed the most recent injustice. An alternative framing would be that he needed to develop his skills more fully, or that the person they chose was better than he was, or that maybe he really didn't know why he didn't get chosen, and it might be smart to seek advice from senior people to tell him where he fell short so that he could work on improving in these areas.

He found it easier to stew about the unfairness of it rather than take the more uncomfortable path of figuring out how he needed to improve. After a period of soul-searching, he pushed himself to have a long talk with his boss. They did a post-mortem. Together, they identified two or three skill areas for improvement and agreed on a game plan for him to work on those areas. Eighteen months later, when another full producer job became available, he was chosen for the position.

Injustice becomes part of your life experience and impacts your narratives. For this reason, I urge people who have suffered a trauma that they experience as an injustice to take time out to process it. You need to reflect on what just happened, seek advice from others who witnessed it, and figure out whether you played a role in what happened. An injustice won't kill you—and you can't avoid injustice—but you do need to learn from it so that you can keep it from happening again. Learning the wrong lesson, or failing to learn a lesson at all, may doom you to repeat some version of the same experience.

The Cost of Failing to Process Injustice

I frequently meet people who experience enough injustice that they begin to feel like victims. They don't take the time to reflect on their experiences, seek advice, learn valuable lessons, and make course adjustments. As a result, they become accident-prone or even gun-shy. Worse, they learn lessons that help ensure they will not reach their potential. For example, they decide it's wiser to look out for themselves and do things only if they receive explicit credit. By taking this approach, they undermine their ability to exhibit character and leadership traits that could help their careers.

This mind-set can create a dangerous and self-defeating downward spiral. You begin to lose faith that justice will prevail. As a result, you fail to take key steps that could help you build your career because you fear that a new injustice will arise. With this attitude, things don't go well, and you create a self-fulfilling prophecy. As a result, you get angrier, more frustrated, and ever more convinced that the deck is stacked against you.

Make the time to process injustices. Thinking through injustices done to you, and considering how they are impacting your current behavior, is essential to your personal growth and development.

If the injustice is recent, reflect in a sustained way on what happened. Make sure you do enough work to develop key lessons that can be learned from the experience. Review these lessons with friends and loved ones. You must understand that everyone eventually runs into a situation where they feel they've been wronged. Don't beat yourself up over this. Do, however, slow yourself down long enough to learn from the experience.

Being at Your Best

As discussed in chapter 2, as part of understanding your story, it's vital to reflect on situations in which you were at your best.

Interestingly, many of us have a hard time remembering these situations. We can get so caught up in the day-to-day pressures and obligations of our jobs that we forget about those situations in which we were absolutely fabulous. Recalling these situations is critical because you can gain an insight from them that can help guide your actions today.

The Chef Who Got Sick of His Job

I met with a restaurant operator who was taking the "Owner President" course at Harvard. He had originally started a mid-priced Italian restaurant on the West Coast and over the years had expanded to three locations. Like many people attending that executive education program, he was hoping to improve his leadership and business skills and to use the time to reflect on whether he wanted to make some changes in his life and career. He started by telling me that he was getting sick of running restaurants.

I asked him why.

"First, it's getting tougher to be a small business owner," he said. "Insurance costs and health care costs are rising. As we've grown, there are more management issues to deal with, and there are more administrative issues generally. I feel like I'm working harder just to keep up, and sometimes I feel like I'm getting squeezed in a vise."

The chef's father and paternal grandfather had been successful business executives. They were not thrilled with his decision to attend culinary school, become a chef, and open a restaurant. He observed that it wasn't easy for him being the third generation of his family living in the same town. Although he loved his father and grandfather—both still alive—they directly and indirectly put a lot of pressure on him, and he often felt he couldn't live up to their expectations.

His father had a dominant personality. "He thinks he's an authority on everything," the chef told me, "and needs to have the last word on most matters." This attitude might have worked with his father's subordinates, but it did not sit very well with his own son.

I asked him to try to forget about the current situation for a few minutes and recall a situation in which he felt at his best and felt great about what he was doing. "I'll have to think about that," he said. "OK, it was when I was running my first restaurant about ten years ago. We were smaller then. I got a thrill every day from creating dishes and serving customers. I do love to come up with new dishes, I love meeting the patrons, and I love the atmosphere of a restaurant. I'm good at it, and I think we help put a smile on people's faces. For me, it's really a blessing to be able to do this work." He was beaming.

"So, why were you just talking about being sick of running a restaurant? And how'd you get yourself stuck in this current situation?"

He laughed. Building three restaurants with a large number of employees felt like a "big deal—it made me feel like more of a success." He then got quiet for a minute. "Damn it, I must admit that I probably added new locations to impress my father, and maybe folks in the community. I was looking for ways to get the monkey off my back—I was tired of feeling I had to prove something. Ironically, running three restaurants hasn't proved a damn thing, other than it's a pain in the neck!"

As a result of this discussion, he began to believe that it was important for him to get back to feeling great about what he was doing. In this case, it meant spending more of his time thinking about food, interacting with his customers, and simply enjoying the atmosphere of the restaurant. It also meant putting on hold identifying new real estate locations, planning new sites, or growing any larger. Fortunately, the core management group of his operations had great mutual respect and shared the same objectives. They wanted to produce good food, make customers happy, and focus on quality versus quantity.

Ultimately, the restaurant operator was able to reallocate his time and put more focus on what he enjoyed. He learned to delegate more of the tasks he didn't enjoy. He reported back nine months later and told me he was enjoying his work much more. In particular, he was pleased to have reoriented his activities and dropped some of the baggage he had been carrying to please others. This progress was helped by his willingness to reflect on how his life story may have created certain insecurities that negatively impacted his decision making. He also reflected more on which of his life experiences had involved high performance and created a sense of fulfillment for him. This exercise helped him become much more aware of what stressed him out, what made him happy, and what helped him perform at a high level.

I urge you to do this exercise as part of understanding your life story. You may not have thought about this for some time, and it can give you great insight into those actions you could take today and in the future to be at your best.

Self-Awareness Versus "Should"

This chapter is about understanding who you are and more fully understanding your actions. You can better understand your actions by more thoroughly understanding your life story. As I've discussed, there are several strands of your story.

Moreover, every experience you have builds your story further and amends the narratives in your head.

Again, I encourage you to do the exercises in this chapter. In addition, I suggest you push yourself to try to understand why you do what you do.

- If you're taking actions that make you unhappy, unfulfilled, or regretful—why? Is there something in your life experience, story, or narratives that could help you understand your actions?

- If you cannot take an action that your best judgment tells you to take, can you zero in on why you are unable to act? Is there something about your story that could help you understand?

The key word in all this is *why*. There is no right answer when it comes to actions that will help you achieve your dreams and reach your potential. It's a matter of trying to understand and decipher why you're doing what you're doing. The more you practice this, the better you will become at understanding yourself.

The Role of Self-Understanding

The effort to assess your skills, understand your passions, and take several of the actions discussed in the next chapters will be much easier if you begin the process of more fully understanding yourself. I say "begin" because you will not complete this task overnight. It will require practice and time.

You may know what you're supposed to do, but you just can't bring yourself to do it—and you may not know why. Often, the impediment goes deeper than the intellectual understanding. You must understand the internal impediments that are keeping you from taking certain actions. These obstacles may be as formidable as a brick wall sitting in the middle of a highway. If this is the case, you may feel that you just can't seem to move forward. You are stuck.

If this sounds like you, focus on the advice in this chapter to better understand yourself. This effort is hard work but should ultimately pay big dividends. This work, as well as the suggestions of the previous chapters, constitutes the major base you're building for reaching your potential. In chapters 5 through 8, you will build on this foundation and learn strategies for pursuing your dream, improving your job performance, and then going the extra mile to reach your potential.

Suggested Follow-Up Steps

- Select one or more friends with whom to discuss your respective life stories. Each of you should come to the session with your basic life story written down. Reflect on what you learn from these discussions.

- Using the drafts of your success and failure narratives, consider what circumstances cause one of these narratives to be present in your mind. Can you recall an important decision that was influenced by one of these narratives? Why did that happen?

- Author a story of your future. Write down the story of your life that you'd like to tell ten or twenty years from now. Make sure to include details of your specific jobs, your life, and other important activities. What do you learn from this exercise?

CHAPTER FIVE

Making the Most of Your Opportunities

Performance and Career Management

- Have you thought about a dream job that could uniquely suit your skills and passions?
- Do you have a plan for achieving this dream?
- Do senior people in your organization know what you're doing and what you want?
- Do you focus your time and energy on the three most important drivers of high performance in your current job?
- Are you in a marathon or a sprint?

Once you've tackled the subjects of the previous chapters—once you've established a process for assessing your strengths and weaknesses, gained a greater awareness of what you enjoy, and worked to understand yourself better—it is time to turn to more practical considerations. How do you apply the insights you've gained to the challenge of performing at a high level and managing your career? Reaching your potential is not like throwing a switch and turning on a lightbulb. Rather, it is an integrated process that requires you to reflect, learn in a disciplined way, and translate your insights into actions. Through this iterative process, you will improve your ability to be at your best and make the most of potential career opportunities.

Taking on the Challenge: Communication, Analysis, and Focus

In this chapter, we discuss the importance of thinking about potential jobs that best match your skills and your passions. You will learn about the importance of communicating with current and potential employers regarding your job aspirations. Although you might like to believe that employers can discern what's in your mind, the truth is that they can't unless you speak up.

This chapter also discusses how to zero in on the key success factors of your job and apply your talents to excelling along those dimensions. We'll discuss the importance of focusing on actions that are likely to improve your performance rather than being unduly distracted by office politics and inside gossip about how to get ahead at your firm.

Because the world, your industry, your company, and you are constantly changing, this chapter also discusses how to update your thinking regularly with a clean sheet of paper.

Finally, I discuss potential approaches to managing yourself when things go poorly. How should you react to setbacks? Do they signal that you've done something wrong, are in the wrong job, or need to radically rethink your career? Or are you in danger of overreacting to setbacks that are bound to occur and, while traumatic, are par for the course?

Do You Think About a Dream Job?

Almost everyone I meet has at least one ideal job in their minds, whether or not they are consciously focused on it. This position usually involves a big leap beyond where the person is now. Even though it may be a stretch —likely requiring several more years of experience and skill development—the person believes that this job could ultimately be an excellent match between his or her capabilities and passions.

When you're sitting in the park, on vacation, or lying awake at night, is there a job you think about ultimately doing? Do you daydream about how it might feel to do that job?

Take out a piece of paper, and try writing down the details of your dream job. Aspects of this job may be role specific, such as being your own boss, running your own business, or becoming a CEO. Or it may involve identifying certain tasks you love to perform. Alternatively, it may relate to a cause you care deeply about. Ideally, it is likely to be a good potential match between your abilities and your passions.

Writing down your dream is an important step forward. It helps you visualize the key elements of an ideal job. It can be the essential extra step that will help you recognize and jump on a new opportunity you might otherwise let slip away—either because you hadn't previously considered it or weren't quick enough to move.

Making an Unlikely Career Move

A friend of mine had two seemingly unrelated aspirations: working on environmental matters and also running an organization. The dream of running an organization seemed more realistic than the conservationist dream because he was working in the financial services industry at the time. How he could move from a financial services job to working on environmental matters?

On several occasions, he had spoken to his superiors about his personal interest in environmental matters. As a result, when his firm decided to establish a sustainability practice, they asked him if he'd like to head it up. In this new role, he would keep his existing responsibilities but also be the firm's point person for talking to natural resource and energy-related firms about how to achieve their objectives in an environmentally sustainable fashion. The company provided this service not because they thought it would be lucrative but because they believed it would be franchise-enhancing and might indirectly lead to incremental business opportunities.

My friend said yes to this unexpected assignment, figuring that he would deepen his knowledge of sustainability matters while he continued with his banking career. A few years later, apparently out of the blue, a large sustainability-related nonprofit invited him to interview for its newly open job of CEO. His recent experience at his firm, as well as his leadership skills, made him a strong candidate. He jumped at the chance to interview and ultimately was selected. His passion for the nonprofit's mission, as well as his skills and domain knowledge, helped him land the position.

Against what seemed to be long odds, he was now in a job that addressed two of his professional dreams. How did it happen? It wasn't a straight line or a clear path, but he navigated the journey successfully because he had thought about his dream job and was quick to pounce on opportunities that might help him pursue it.

If you haven't done so already, take a stab at writing down your dream job. Let yourself daydream. For the moment, give the critical and analytical part of your brain a rest—and don't try to figure out how in the world you're going to get from where you are now to your desired position. This exercise is an essential first step that should help you gain a greater degree of self-awareness. It also puts you in a position to take ownership of the important intermediate steps necessary to pursue your dream.

The Importance of Speaking Up

Once you have a better sense of your dream job, you should explore whether this job is actually available at your current company. If so, can you navigate within your company to achieve your dream—or, at least, get closer to achieving that dream?

You may believe that your boss or other senior people know you well enough to understand how your skills fit with your passions. However, you need to realize that, unfortunately, senior people at your firm are not psychic. They are not able to read your mind. Further, they likely have many other responsibilities to worry about. As a result, they expect you to take responsibility for communicating to them what you want, and they expect you to have given some thought to the potential job assignments that might help you get there.

Many professionals are reluctant to share their dream job with senior people at their firm. Are you one of them? Why? Maybe you're afraid that your current boss will feel offended that your dream job is not in his or her area. Maybe you fear that your boss will see you as disloyal if you express your desire to do something else. Maybe you feel that no one at the company really cares what you want, and so you should keep your aspirations to yourself. You may believe that senior people at your firm are very wise and have an unusual knack for picking the right people for the right jobs. If they believed you were a good fit for a job, they'd certainly have asked you—right? You may feel awkward talking about your needs and desires. You may feel that it is self-indulgent, even selfish. Finally, you may be afraid that people at your firm will laugh at you and will see your aspirations as being ridiculous. Do any of these justifications for keeping silent strike a chord?

A Dream of Latin America

A highly talented senior executive who worked at a large industrial company headquartered in Europe was at Harvard for an executive program and came to see me about her career. She said she was discouraged in her current job and upset with her firm. I asked why.

She told me that an opportunity to run a business unit in Latin America had just been given to a colleague. She believed she was far more qualified than the person selected. Worst of all, she didn't even hear about the opportunity until the announcement of the new appointment. "It's one thing to interview me for the job and choose someone else," she said. "It's another thing to not even bother to speak with me about the opportunity! Do they think so little of me? I thought I was doing a superb job at this company!"

She was seriously thinking about quitting once she returned to the firm at the conclusion of the training class. She even pulled out a draft of a resignation e-mail she was thinking about sending her boss.

I listened to the story, read the e-mail, and told her to slow down. First, I asked if she had informed her boss that she would have liked to have been offered this job.

"No," she replied. "I was too angry, and I wanted to wait until I calmed down before speaking with him. But I'm sure he must know."

"Why are you sure he must know?"

She reflected for a moment and said that although she couldn't cite a specific conversation, she was certain he knew what she wanted.

"Here's a shocker for you," I said. "He may not even have thought of it. Judging from all you've said, if I were your boss, I don't think I would have thought of it. You're doing well, your reviews are excellent, and you seem to have a very bright future. The signals you've sent so far indicate you love what you're doing right now. I like to think I'm in touch with the people I manage, and I think I would have made the same omission as your boss. Additionally, it's not obvious to me why this would have been the ideal next move for you. Why do you believe this was the right job for you?"

She explained that her mother was from Latin America and that she had many relatives in the region. She had dreamed of someday returning there as head of a business.

"Does your boss know this?" I asked. "Have you told people at the company about your family background and desires?"

She stopped and, after a few seconds, smiled a little sheepishly. She realized she'd never told her boss this story. A couple of her peers and subordinates knew, but it was highly probable that senior folks at the firm had little idea about this part of her background.

"If this was so important to you, why the heck did you keep it to yourself?" I asked.

"Well, I'm not sure. I just never explicitly explained all this to senior people, although I thought a few were aware of my background. Also, things had been going so well for the past twelve years, and I didn't want to make waves by asking for a new job."

We both burst out laughing. "So, let me get this straight," I said. "You don't want to make waves? You mean, like quitting suddenly?"

After we stopped laughing, we agreed that the onus was on her to explain her dream. The senior people at her company were not omniscient. It was more than a little unrealistic for her to assume that they knew what she was thinking if she didn't actually tell them.

Based on this reality check, she went back to her company and sat down with her boss and other senior people. She explained her dream. She reported back to me that they were highly sympathetic and enthusiastic about helping her achieve it. About fifteen months later, an even more senior position in Latin America became available. She was offered the job and immediately accepted. Ironically, the person in the first job reported to her in this new role.

She learned a valuable lesson: she needed to own the responsibility for communicating upward.

Am I Being Too Political?

Many people tell me they're hesitant to do much communicating upward. They view it as political. They bristle when they think their peers are playing up to the bosses and trying to spend time with senior people. One young man said to me, "I hate that game. I promised myself I would get ahead on merit and not resort to buttering up the boss. I keep my head down and do my job!"

"Communicating what you're doing and who you are is part of the job," I said.

From a manager's perspective, it is valuable to know what your people are doing and what they're thinking. Simply stated, senior people don't know what they don't know. I always encouraged my direct reports to communicate with me sufficiently so that I would know what they thought I needed to know about them. Although I worked hard to regularly schedule time with them and ask questions, I also was keenly aware that there might be questions I didn't have the presence of mind to ask.

If you believe your primary job is to avoid making waves and that your work should speak for itself, I urge you to rethink that assumption. If you have this belief, I don't think you're defining your job expansively enough. Please consider that you may be using this mind-set as a crutch because speaking up makes you uncomfortable. Yes, you have to decide how much upward communication is too much, but you need to recognize that some amount is necessary. You don't necessarily need to go out for drinks with the boss, but you do need to schedule time (or use the time he or she schedules with you) to explain what you're working on, who you are, and what you want. You need to *own* this.

The Top Three Tasks

As discussed in chapter 2, I often see talented individuals who don't fully understand the needs of their current job. This is one of the most common reasons highly skilled, passionate people fail to live up to their potential. They may be in the right job, but they haven't done enough analysis to make the most of the opportunity. Sometimes I see these people moving from one job to another, consistently underperforming based on their potential. They're not quite sure why.

Can you write down on a piece of paper the top three tasks that you must do extremely well to succeed in your job? Most folks I speak with respond very quickly and generically—but their answers suggest that they have not fully considered the question. Many people fail to recognize the need to do this analysis, particularly when they move to a new job. This analysis is just as important when the move is a promotion within your company.

The Newly Promoted Product Manager

I was speaking with a product manager at a leading global consumer goods company. Previously an assistant product manager, he had been recently promoted to full product manager for one of his company's emerging products. He believed this wasn't a big leap because he had apprenticed as an assistant for a number of years. I asked how it was going.

"Not so well," he replied. He explained that his reviews were weaker than before.

I asked what his bosses were identifying as his strengths and his weaknesses.

"Well, I'm still getting high marks for my technical skills," he said. "But my bosses are starting to criticize my judgment." In particular, he had been faulted for some of his strategic judgments and tactical product management decisions.

I asked him to describe the three key tasks he needed to do well in this job. He answered by recalling the top tasks he had needed to do well in his previous job.

"Are those still the same in this current position?" I asked.

"Sure," he said. "A product manager is a product manager."

I was no expert on the needs of his job, but I pressed him, asking if he was certain about his answer. For example, the product had changed and, therefore, the consumer dynamics were likely to be different. Didn't this mean that the drivers of product success might be different? In addition, he now managed a team, whereas before, he was a team member. Had he taken for granted many of the key team-leadership tasks that had been performed by his former boss? Could he identify those tasks? Finally, I suggested that he carefully examine the reasons for the key judgment and tactical criticisms he was receiving. Did he understand what they were?

He went back to his firm and spent several weeks talking to people, focusing on what made someone great in his current position. He discovered that, even though he thought he understood the requirements of the job, he hadn't been sufficiently deliberate in defining them. He began to realize that managing product innovation was a much bigger challenge in his current job. He realized he needed to be much more focused on doing more product testing, R&D, focus groups with customers, and the like, because the rate of competitive innovation in this space was much higher than with his previous product.

He also realized that recruiting, training, and coaching his staff were more crucial in this job. His previous boss had spent a great deal of time on this. He now realized he had unwittingly given these tasks short shrift. As a result, his team was weaker, less coordinated, and less effective. He started to understand it would be tough to succeed in this job without having a strong team whose members worked well together.

Finally, he learned that criticisms he received about his judgment were closely related to those concerning his management style. His bosses were observing that he didn't spend sufficient time on the right issues, and he reacted to problems that came up rather than proactively anticipate them. Essentially, they were criticizing him for not being on top of the three main tasks necessary for superb performance in his job.

Fortunately, he took the criticisms to heart and had a dramatically better second year in his new job. He learned that focusing on these top tasks meant the difference between mediocre and outstanding performance.

He loved his new job, and his skills were a good fit for it. However, he learned that passion and skills alone weren't enough to ensure success. He needed to do a basic analysis of the key success factors of the job so that he could excel. Once he took these steps, he vaulted to a new level of performance.

Have the Needs of Your Current Job Changed?

Let's say you've done this analysis, and now you're on your way to performing at a higher level. Things are going well. Life is good.

Then something happens. The world changes, the industry changes, your company culture changes, or maybe there's an issue in an adjacent business unit. Maybe a few of your key people quit. Maybe you change. Maybe the company grows, and you are struggling to adapt.

For better or worse, things do change—and when they do, you must adapt. The problem is that changes often occur gradually over a period of years until they reach a tipping point. You may not even be aware of the changes, and, as a result, they appear to sneak up on you. It's almost as if one day you wake up, and things are suddenly not going well. How did it happen so fast? What went wrong?

How a Salesman Can Become a Dinosaur

A technology company salesman was responsible for covering many of his firm's most important customers. He had done this job successfully for many years. His company had started by selling a single innovative product. Over the years, it introduced several product extensions that helped fuel its growth.

After a sustained period of profitable growth and success, one of the company's direct competitors introduced an innovative product that threatened the company's dominance in this space. In addition, the way customers used this type of technology had been gradually changing in recent years. These changes were due to product innovations, as well as advances in internet, mobile computing, and platform technologies.

Against this backdrop, the salesman's boss sat down with him and informed him that the company had decided to take away some of his key customers and give them to another salesperson.

"Why?" he asked. It didn't make sense—he had great customer relationships.

His boss explained that the needs of the job had changed. His role now required much more ability to solve customer problems and work with the firm's technical people to address customer needs.

Ironically, the salesman had the aptitude to adapt to these changes. He had an engineering degree as well as good product and system aptitude. His job was being downsized because he hadn't taken the initiative to adapt to the changes going on in the industry, across technologies, and among his customers. His boss could evaluate only the performance he observed and had concluded that the salesman had limited capability and growth potential.

Why had this happened? The harsh reality was that he had gotten so comfortable doing the job the way he had always done it that he never took the initiative to study and update his views regarding the critical task needs of the sales position. He assumed the company would push him to update his skills if it believed it was necessary, and he didn't think this was his responsibility. As a result, he had failed to spend a sufficiently high percentage of his time on those key tasks that were now essential to superb performance.

Again, it's not as if he was incapable of doing this analysis. When he first started, he had made a careful analysis of the job's needs and adapted his behavior and skill development accordingly. Unfortunately, as the world changed, he stopped updating this analysis and slacked off on his attendance at company training sessions intended to help him serve his customer needs.

"Things were going well," he reflected. "My customers loved me. The company loved me. I kind of prided myself on being a bit eccentric, and maybe a lone wolf who didn't need to go to training sessions. When I did attend, I didn't pay careful attention and follow up on what I learned. I was a star salesman—I didn't *need* to."

He now had a crucial choice to make. Should he pout about losing half of his accounts? Or should he rededicate himself to studying the needs of the job and adapting his skill development and time allocation to addressing those needs?

He still had a good deal of his career ahead of him. He loved the company and the job. He believed the job was still a good fit for his skills. Because he wanted to stay in the job, he decided to update his views of the top three tasks critical to his performance. Then he took advantage of the company's excellent training programs to improve his portfolio of skills. He found that he enjoyed learning and updating his repertoire. In his daily work, he began to track his time rigorously to make sure he was spending it on the most important tasks.

A year later he reported back to me that he'd been reinstated to several of the accounts he had lost. Clearly, his boss was impressed with the way he had responded to this shot across the bow. He regretted that he had waited for a setback to update his understanding of the needs of the job and adapt his actions accordingly. He vowed never to repeat this same mistake. Fortunately, he was now again on track to furthering his career and reaching his potential.

The Clean Sheet of Paper

Assuming you're in the right job, here are a few steps that will help you stay current in addressing the top tasks critical to being successful:

- Do a clean-sheet-of-paper exercise for your current job. If you were starting the job now, what would be the three tasks most critical to being superb? If it's helpful, consider interviewing peers and customers to answer this question.

- Assess how your current skills line up with those task requirements. What training or further skills development do you need? Focus on a plan to update your skills.

- Make sure that your time allocation matches these top tasks. Track your time for two weeks, and determine whether the time spent matches with the top three critical tasks. Assess the reasons for the match or mismatch. Develop a plan for focusing at least 70 percent of your time on these key tasks. To achieve this match, consider delegating nonpriority tasks or learning to say no much more frequently. Keep a list of the three tasks on your wall, and look at them before you agree to demands on your time.

These are basic steps that most of us (including me) get lazy about doing. Focus on updating this work periodically.

Only You Can Derail Yourself

A career is a marathon, not a sprint. Developing skills, following your passion, and matching your efforts to the job are great, but they will take you only so far. It also helps to have a mindset that anticipates occasional setbacks and prepares you to pick yourself up and dust yourself off, reflect on what happened, and then move forward.

Whether you work for someone else or run your own company, it takes a lot of emotional and physical energy to consistently drive to improve and build your skills and to attack your work with intensity. No matter how well you fit the job, there will inevitably be elements that annoy, discourage, and wear on you.

There are many examples of such potential irritants: your boss is a jerk, you got passed over for promotion, your compensation is lower than you expected, you had a bad year, or you don't like one of your peers, subordinates, or clients. You feel tired and worn out, you have problems at home, one of your kids is sick. The company culture has changed, the way the company makes money has changed, regulation negatively impacts the business, there's a severe recession, and so on. You get the idea.

These challenges happen, and when they do, they can sap your strength and emotional energy. Worse, they can take the fun out of your job. Now what?

A key competence in making the most of your opportunities is the ability to keep your balance, reflect, and find ways to reinvigorate yourself so that you can move forward. Unfortunate events, injustices, and other people's behavior can trip you up. To weather these setbacks and challenges, it helps to have the mind-set that only you can derail yourself. You are the captain of this journey. As captain, you want to spend time thinking about a philosophy for dealing with annoyances, setbacks, and adversity. Thinking about it in advance will help you deal with it when it occurs.

Dealing with a Painful Setback

I received an urgent phone call from a former colleague who had just found out he wasn't being promoted. His boss told him he wasn't going to become managing director this year, but he had a good chance for promotion next year.

He called me to discuss what happened. In finishing the story, he also explained how he reacted to the news: "I told off my boss and stormed out of the office. I was so angry. I worked so hard for this. My boss says he argued on my behalf, but that doesn't make me any less angry. I feel embarrassed in front of my peers. My wife was going to have a little cocktail reception for me after I got promoted, and now she's embarrassed about having to tell her friends not to come over for drinks. It's just awful."

I asked him, "Do you still enjoy the job? Do you still like the firm? Do you trust the senior people?" Despite being very angry, he answered yes to all those questions.

I advised him to call his boss immediately. "Apologize for your emotional reaction. If possible, do it in person. If you can't bring yourself to do that, work on getting yourself to that point.

"Second, make sure you go right back into the office tomorrow and keep your cool," I added. "Focus on the job. Even though you feel lousy, do your utmost to be highly professional and in good spirits. Next year will come around in a nanosecond, and you want to show you're capable of handling this in a professional manner."

I could see he was annoyed by my advice and was still angry over what had just happened earlier that day. My fear was he was going to let a momentary lapse in his professionalism taint an otherwise superb record. It wasn't his fault he wasn't promoted, but he certainly was responsible for his reaction to the news.

In fact, I was sympathetic because I have been guilty, at times, of reacting emotionally. Over the years, when I was criticized, I sometimes made the mistake of reacting defensively. Maybe it was because I was tired and feeling insecure, or maybe I thought the critique was designed to make me look bad, or maybe I just felt overwhelmed. In almost all of these cases, I later realized that I should have counted to ten, controlled my emotions, focused on the substance of the criticism, and kept my cool.

I have seen numerous cases over the years in which the reaction to a setback was ultimately more damaging than the setback itself. When people are gracious under lousy circumstances, it is impressive. If they blow their top, all people remember is that they couldn't control their emotions, and colleagues wonder if it could happen in other critical situations.

This young man ultimately did seek out his boss and apologize to him. It was not easy. However, his boss was impressed that he had the fortitude to come back in and be gracious. He was promoted the next year. No one at his firm remembers which year he made managing director—or that he was initially passed over. His wife has forgotten, too.

What's the point of this story? Again, your career is a long haul, not a short sprint. If you think you're going to get through it without being humiliated, feeling embarrassed, being treated unfairly, or having something bad happen to you, you're being unrealistic. The trick is not to avoid these setbacks. Instead, it lies in learning to deal with them.

Dealing with Injustice

In learning to deal with disappointment, I find it useful to think about how you've handled past injustice. Chapter 4 described an exercise regarding a past injustice. This exercise can give you a window into the reasons for your own behavior and provide insight into the best way to deal with future challenges.

Reaching your potential is not about avoiding injustice. Unfortunately, you can't and won't. Instead, it's about how you deal with injustice. Do you blame others? Blow your top? Withdraw? If so, do you understand why? Do you step back and reflect on what you can learn from what happened, or do you try to block it out of your mind because it's too painful to think about? Do you become gun-shy?

I don't have a simple, catchall answer for how you should deal with injustice. However, I believe there are a few steps you should take when dealing with a setback.

- Keep your cool. Don't take a rash action that you might later regret. Don't let your immediate intense emotions lead you into an ill-advised action. There is usually time to act. Make sure you take action after you let your mind and good judgment come to the fore.

- Take time to reflect. That may mean waiting for an evening or a weekend, or until you can take a week's vacation. Work to get some perspective on what happened. In particular, what are you going to learn from what happened? Is there something you could have done differently that you would like to address in the future?

- Get outside help if needed. This will likely mean turning to people with whom you have close relationships for support, advice, and perspective (see chapter 7).

Passion is essential to your success. The risk is that great passion can overflow in a difficult situation. You want to manage your emotions, act judiciously, and learn from setbacks.

A Rush to Judgment

One reason people fail to use their skills to make the most of their opportunities—and therefore fail to reach their potential—is the short time horizon they use to think about their careers.

An outstanding technology executive came to see me for advice. She had been in an executive position at her company for about three months. She took the job after a successful stint at an advertising firm. She was not enjoying her new job at all. In fact, she said, up to this point she hated her job. She explained that the culture was different from what she had expected. The firm was founded and run by engineering and software experts, and the culture was product-driven and technically oriented. She had a general knowledge of technology and was learning the firm's products, but she couldn't go toe-to-toe with the other executives on these issues. She felt like an outsider.

She added that she couldn't figure out how to add value to the company. As a result, she had begun to speak with executive search firms and had already been on two job interviews. Maybe taking this current job had been a big mistake, she reasoned, and it would be best to correct it quickly. Psychologically, she was tolerating each day in her current job only because she knew in the back of her mind she was going to leave soon. As a result, she started to slack off on getting to know her peers and understanding the business. This, in turn, made the job even less enjoyable. She had mentally checked out.

She said she was in my office looking for advice, but my impression was that she was really looking for me to validate what she was doing.

I asked her to back up a bit and explain why she took the technology job in the first place. She explained she thought she would love the industry, the product provided substantial value to customers, she liked the people, and she thought she could offer a lot of consumer and product marketing expertise to the company.

"What's changed?"

"Well," she said, "I think I just explained that to you."

"You've told me you feel like an outsider and aren't able to fit into the culture. I want to know what aspects of your initial premise have changed."

She was silent.

I told her I didn't know enough to give her clear and specific advice. I didn't know the people, and she was the one who had to live in this situation. I did know enough to say that cultural adaptation often takes a while—often as much as a full year.

We all take for granted that our first year as a junior person will involve a certain amount of culture shock. To deal with this, most companies offer various types of programs aimed at "onboarding" entry-level hires. The truth is that moving laterally is no less a culture shock, and it often takes even more time and effort.

My two cents' worth of advice to this visitor was that, as unhappy as she was, she really didn't know yet whether this job was a fit. It didn't sound to me as if there was an obvious event or element of the job that made this clear—yet. She still trusted the CEO and other senior managers. She still thought they needed her skills. She still was intrigued by the job's needs and the skill fit.

I suggested that she consider resetting the clock in her mind. "Give it one year," I said. "If after one year you still feel the same way, fine—quit with few regrets." Nine more months wasn't going to matter in the grand scheme of things, I told her. In future interviews, moreover, it would be easier to explain that she gave the job a year, as opposed to abruptly quitting after only three or four months.

She reported back to me a year later. I was pleasantly surprised to hear how enthusiastic she had become about her job. She now said she loved it. She had almost forgotten how unhappy she had been when she came to visit me. What changed? After leaving my office a year earlier, she put all her emotional energy into doing the job and integrating into the culture. After a few months, she began to find her rhythm and started to see how she could add value. She began to develop close relationships. She better understood the culture. She started to feel like an insider.

I could tell numerous stories like this one. They underscore the point that calibrating your time horizon is crucial to reaching your potential. Relationships and adaptation take time. If your internal clock is ticking like a time bomb, it's tough to focus on the key actions you must take to integrate into a new job and build your skills.

The Clock in Your Head

There is always a clock in our heads, although we are seldom consciously aware of its influence on our thoughts. How old am I? How should I be doing at this age? How are my peers doing?

How does this job fit with other priorities in my life? How long do I want to work? These are only a few of the time-related questions we constantly ask ourselves. These questions can be exacerbated by the failure scenario that is sometimes present in our minds (discussed in chapter 4).

In an effort to help you discern your passions, I suggested in a previous chapter that you ask yourself what you would do if you had only a year to live. However, once you have made a job choice based on your best judgment, you need to then slow down and give it time. It takes at least a year, or even more, to judge cultural fit—barring the emergence of a significant ethical issue, of course. In many careers, the early years as a junior person are a pain in the neck—but climbing the next rung up the ladder allows you to delegate more menial tasks, have more fun, and really shine, if you stick around long enough to get to this point.

If you mentally have one foot out the door, you aren't likely to apply your skills and passions to finding out how good you can be in your current role. Creating artificial deadlines and time pressure can derail an otherwise promising career. Everyone matures at a different pace. In fact, in numerous cases, I have seen people take several years to grow and mature before they develop into superbly effective executives.

Be aware of the clock in your head. Use the mental models and exercises discussed earlier in this book to assess your passions and make a wise job decision. However, once you've made that choice, promise yourself to give it sufficient time. After a sufficient period of time has passed, then reassess.

I have been asked many times how I was able to stay with one firm for twenty-two years. My response has always been the same: one year at a time. I didn't decide to do the job for three years, or even two; instead, I gave it one year and then regularly reassessed. During that year, I put all my energy into being at my best in my job. If I was miserable on some days or weeks, I knew that at the end of the year I would take time to assess my situation. I didn't waste time or emotional energy deciding whether I was "in" or "out."

Ask yourself what time frame is in your mind regarding your current job. Are you spending too much time deciding whether to stay or go? Do you take calls from search firms and actually go to interviews? Why? Think about how these actions might be impacting your performance and your efforts to be at your best.

High Performance: Be at Your Best in What You've Chosen

Much of this book is about you and addresses how you can better understand yourself.

This work is critical, but, ultimately, what you do matters. Over the years, I have known many talented people who failed to perform at their best and later regretted wasting attractive opportunities. At some point in their careers, they stopped acting with a degree of urgency and motivation to improve their job performance. Their passion for the work was still there, but their dedication to being a student of the job began to wane. This dedication, in some cases, was impacted by a work-related setback, by a habit of taking the job for granted, by complacency about their performance, or by distractions outside work. These reactions are natural, but career ambivalence is an issue you should be alert to.

You need to focus on doing a good job at what's right in front of you. If it fits your passions and skills, that's great, but there's still a lot more that goes into performing at a high level in your job. Communicating upward, updating the needs of the job, and managing yourself are all critical—and often overlooked—aspects of reaching your potential.

Once you have mastered the material in the first five chapters of this book, you need to go the extra mile and turn your attention to additional factors that make the difference between good and great. We'll examine these issues in the next several chapters.

Suggested Follow-Up Steps

- When was the last time you spoke to your immediate boss or other senior person at your company regarding your job and career aspirations? If it has been a while, consider raising these points in a coaching session or your year-end review.

- Commit to doing a regular analysis of the top three tasks that are critical to success in your current job. Track your time, and make sure it matches closely with performing those tasks. Make sure you are focusing your skill development on being better able to perform those tasks, and surround yourself with people who are able to complement your abilities.

- Write down the impediments to being at your best in your current job. Make a list of the distractions or other factors that seem to be diverting you from being superb.

CHAPTER SIX

Good Versus Great

Character and Leadership

- Do you work to figure out what you believe, and do you have the courage to act on those beliefs?
- Do you act like an owner in your job?
- Do you play the game with some degree of abandon?
- Do you clearly know your values and ethical boundaries?

It is a challenge to know your strengths and weaknesses, understand your passions, understand yourself, and then apply this knowledge to being at your best in a specific job and to managing your career. If you can do these things, you'll dramatically increase the likelihood of reaching your potential. All this will get you to a certain point—but you can still go much further. This next step involves examining your character and leadership behaviors.

A Star Wants to Realize His Potential

I worked with a talented professional who made great strides in a large financial services firm. He was promoted to managing director in his mid-thirties. He was well liked by clients, dedicated to his job, and highly valued by his firm for his many commercial contributions. He loved the markets and truly enjoyed solving complex problems for clients. He was a student of the key success factors of his job and enjoyed learning, improving his skills, and adapting to changes in the business. He had found a home professionally.

Then a weird thing happened: he started to crave a greater professional challenge. He approached the senior people in his division and explained his desires. In response, they urged him to keep doing what he was doing. Dissatisfied, he assumed he hadn't been sufficiently specific and forceful and further explained that he wanted to run a business unit. They made it clear that they didn't believe this would be his highest and best contribution to the firm. They said he could continue to have a great career covering clients and being a highly paid producer. Moreover, they believed he should be satisfied with his current role.

He came to visit me to discuss this situation. "Maybe I'm just having a midlife crisis," he mused. "I should be happy with what I have. But I'm only forty-one, and I just can't accept that this is all I'm going to accomplish in my career. The senior folks at my firm keep slamming the door on what I want. I can't figure out why. I thought they loved me. My reviews are outstanding, but I can't get a straight answer from my boss to explain why he won't consider giving me a bigger leadership job."

I encouraged him to go back and dig into his latest review and study his notes from it. To do this, he needed to speak with his boss, ask him to again explain the quantitative results, and also provide a refresher on the verbal comments. I also encouraged him to focus his boss on discussing those categories that dealt specifically with teamwork, his work as a role model, his coaching capabilities, and other leadership attributes.

He proceeded to have these discussions. He learned, to his embarrassment, that he hadn't focused at all on these categories during his year-end review. He realized the ratings in these qualitative categories were relatively low, and there were several negative comments about his coaching of young people (or lack of it). These issues didn't seem to have any impact on his pay and promotion prospects, so he hadn't paid much attention. In his current job, he believed that serving clients and producing business were the only truly important measures of success, and therefore he spent almost none of his time on recruiting, training, coaching, and similar activities. Further, he viewed these activities as the purview of Human Resources or others in the firm who weren't as stellar in production as he was. His bosses did nothing to discourage this view. For all these reasons, he was fairly certain that he was paid at the top of his peer group.

I had seen this type of situation before, so I wasn't really surprised. There was no question that he was great in his job, but he defined that job very narrowly. Of course the firm needed big producers—but to succeed, it also needed leaders who helped make others better. Up to this point in his career, he had behaved as if he had no interest in the latter.

Did he want to be a big producer for the rest of his career, or did he want a broader job? He could do well either way. What was his definition of success, in terms of his legacy, passion, and reaching his potential? He had to decide. I cautioned him that if he chose the path of a broader job, he would have to make several substantial changes in his behavior:

- He would have to be much more unselfish. He would need to think and act as if he were an owner of the firm. He would have to work on recruiting new hires as well as training, coaching, and advising young people and peers—even though he might not get any apparent credit for it. He would have to engage in these activities because that's what leaders do. They act like they own the place and therefore define their jobs very broadly.

- He would have to start operating as a role model for broad leadership behaviors. He would need to be less cynical about firm programs, compliance, and risk management. Why? Because this is what a leader does. It isn't someone else's job.

- He would have to get into the habit of giving credit to others and reducing his own credit-seeking behavior. Up to now, when he secured a piece of business he would take a highly visible victory lap around the firm. That felt great to him, but it turned off all those who had worked on the project along with him. It also implicitly communicated to senior people that, although he was a high-performing producer, he was not a leader.

Unfortunately, his bosses had never previously mentioned these issues to him. Because they viewed him as lacking broad leadership potential, they were happy to define his role more narrowly and were willing to have him keep on doing what he had been doing. They viewed him as filling a role and filling it well and saw no need to alter it. Meanwhile, he never expressed to them a desire to be a leader. In fact, his behavior practically shouted out the opposite message.

"How did I miss this?" he asked me. "I don't want to be just a producer. I want to do more and learn more. It scares me to death that I will look back at my career and say that this was all that I did. Boy, I have really screwed up!"

The toughest part of his situation was that no senior person wanted to take the risk of putting him in a bigger role unless he first was willing to exhibit leadership behaviors. In reality, you often need to act like a leader before people will take the risk of putting you in a broader leadership role.

He realized he would need to do more than just communicate what he wanted. First, he would need to start exhibiting these behaviors in order to build his credibility as a potential leader.

He decided to go after this challenge in earnest. He got involved in entry-level recruiting. He began to coach junior people. It was a struggle for him because he got no discernible credit for these new activities in his compensation package, although he did get a few appreciative pats on the back. He had to retrain himself to do these activities because he wanted to and not for what he hoped to get in return. This was a brutally tough mental shift for him to internalize. It took him a few years.

Ultimately, senior people began to believe that it was worth giving him a chance to lead. They first made him a school recruiting captain—a thankless but important job that, at times, felt to him like a booby prize. After watching him do this job for a while, they then offered him a business unit. He would now have his chance.

The Right Mind-Set

The protagonist in the preceding story was fortunate in several ways. He was so good at production that he got away with not exhibiting leadership and community-building behaviors. Even so, he eventually ran out of gas with this narrow approach. In many other professions, his failure to show leadership and character would have derailed his progress much earlier.

This chapter focuses on the critical role these traits and behaviors play in reaching your potential. They're tough to develop because they're not easy to coach, they may not yield rewards for many years, and they rarely lend themselves to metrics and measurement.

This chapter will discuss what it means to be a leader, act like an owner, and develop a mind-set that helps you exhibit character traits that can vault you to a much higher level of effectiveness.[1] It will also discuss the numerous impediments to reaching this higher level and describe some of the techniques for overcoming these roadblocks.

What Is Leadership?

The words "leader" and "leadership" get tossed around liberally. Despite how often these terms are used, most people aren't sure what they actually mean. If I asked a hundred people to define leadership, I would probably get a hundred different answers.

Let me put forward my own definition. Leadership is the ability to figure out what you believe and then summon the courage to appropriately act on those beliefs. These actions must be geared to adding value to an enterprise and making a positive impact on others.

Based on this definition, I believe there are a multitude of leaders in the world. A single parent, a soldier, a police officer, an entrepreneur, a not-for-profit executive, a manager working in a large company, a college professor, or an employee working in the mailroom—all are potential leaders. I see these leaders every day. They come from every part of the world and every walk of life.

These people figure out what they believe and have the courage to act on those beliefs. They focus on adding value to others. They define their roles broadly and act like owners of their organizations.

By this definition, you don't need to manage anyone to be a leader. Following the same reasoning, you could manage thousands of people and not be a leader—maybe a good manager, but not a leader. It all depends on what you do. You don't need a written invitation to be a leader; it is based on your actions in the context of your situation.

This definition and framing are important. Great organizations, countries, and families are built around a nucleus of people who act as leaders. It's darn near impossible to build a superb and sustainable effort and accomplish something of significance without leadership. I have spent my entire career looking for and developing people who were willing to exhibit these behaviors, and then building businesses and nonprofit organizations around them.

What does this have to do with you? Although I encourage you to follow the prescriptions in the first five chapters of this book, these actions will take you only so far. An essential next step is to use your talents for a greater purpose. When people learn how to do this, they often elevate their game to new and exciting levels that previously were unimaginable to them.

The Importance of Conviction

Step 1 of this effort requires you to figure out what you believe. How hard can that be? For many talented people, it turns out to be extremely difficult.

You can start this effort by adopting a simple lens: put yourself in the shoes of the decision maker, and decide what you would do if you were that person. This is not about figuring out what arguments you would make or playing devil's advocate; instead, it's about actually figuring out how it feels to be in the leader's shoes and agonizing over what you would do in his or her place.

Every day, on our television and computer screens, we see pundits criticizing business and government leaders for their actions—all the while never putting themselves on the hot seat and articulating precisely what they would do if they were in charge. Think of the water cooler talk you hear at work. People second-guess senior management decisions, even though it's anyone's guess what these critics would do if they had the power to decide. It's so much easier to poke holes in others' actions than to go through the stress and soul-searching required when you truly put yourself in the shoes of the decision maker.

In many companies, junior people believe that the path to success is to do their assignments, keep their heads down, and keep their mouths shut. They further believe that it's wise to figure out what the bosses want and work hard to give it to them. To take this logic a step further, it might seem clever to figure out what the boss thinks and then act as if you think it, too; in that way, the boss will think you're really smart. There's an abundance of conventional wisdom rattling around most companies about how to get ahead, and unfortunately it often doesn't include speaking up and making waves.

Great careers and organizations are built on people who are willing to act like leaders. Great organizations depend on people having the guts to speak up—even though the boss may disagree with them, and they may sometimes feel a bit stupid for having opened their mouths. This effort begins with figuring out what you believe and learning to act like an owner.

The Assistant Product Manager Bites His Tongue

An assistant product manager in a consumer products company was working as part of a team on a new product launch. The head of the project was the divisional VP. The team had been working on this launch for several months. The new product would be a brand extension of the firm's highly successful flagship product.

In preparation for the launch, the team held a critical meeting to discuss product features, advertising strategy, and a package of retail trade arrangements that would help market the new product. The proposed trade arrangements included special product displays that retailers could use in their stores. The VP led the discussion, detailing the latest proposals for the key details of the launch. At the end of his comments, he asked the seven professionals in the room if anyone had any comments or disagreed with anything that had been discussed.

The assistant product manager felt a pang of anxiety as he sat silently. He looked around the room and saw no indication that anyone was planning to speak. The VP rephrased his question: "I take it that all of you completely support these plans?" The assistant product manager nodded along with his peers.

As he nodded, he wondered why he felt so uncomfortable. He realized it was because he didn't agree with key elements of the plan. In particular, he didn't like the in-store display, felt the advertising budget should be restructured, and thought the timetable for the launch should also be changed. So why was he nodding?

"I hated myself for just going along with the crowd," he later confessed to me. "But how could I be the only one to disagree with an entire group of people? Plus, it wasn't really my job on the line—it was the divisional VP's responsibility."

The plan proceeded as described. It ultimately encountered several problems, including a number that would have been addressed by the changes the assistant product manager had in his mind during the meeting. He told himself that this wasn't his fault. After all, he was only one member of the team.

In his year-end review, he received solid but not stellar grades. Some of the criticisms focused on his inability to innovate, understand the needs of the trade, and add value on this specific product launch project. The reviewer expressed doubt as to whether the assistant product manager would ever become an outstanding product manager.

He was understandably very upset and alarmed by his review. In the session, he tried to defend himself by detailing some of the steps he might have done differently in the launch. The reviewer asked if he had voiced these suggestions at the time. Of course, he had to admit that he had not. His heart sank as he realized how foolish he sounded in talking about what he might have said but hadn't had the guts to articulate.

He learned a traumatic but valuable lesson: being quiet wasn't as safe as he had previously thought. He promised himself that, in the future, he would push himself much harder to speak up and disagree when appropriate. Great companies seek to develop and promote people who act like owners. This requires an ability to think like a decision maker and have the courage to speak up when appropriate.

Are You Sure It's Not Your Job?

Developing convictions and acting on them are the first big steps in acting like an owner—but they are only first steps. You also have to take the leap to believing that these behaviors are a central part of your job.

I have encountered many professionals who, over the years, reach the conclusion that dealing with thorny organizational issues is simply not their job. They make this distinction in several subtle ways. For example, they claim they don't have the power to address certain important issues. They decide not to stick their necks out to help others. They do only what they get credit for personally. They assert that "people issues" are the province of human resources or some other group or individual. They get caught up in petty interdepartmental rivalries, treating peers in other departments as adversaries. They fail to return phone calls, or they decline to extend themselves to assist people in other divisions because they believe their evaluation and job performance depend primarily on what they do for their own business unit or department.

What do all these actions have in common? They undermine the effectiveness of the company and at the same time narrow the job descriptions of the people exhibiting this behavior. These people are implicitly assuming that justice will not prevail and that it pays to watch out for oneself first and foremost. The problem with this attitude is that it almost always catches up with you. Word begins to get around the company that you're not a leader. This perception damages your ability to attract people to work with you, undermines your job effectiveness, and ultimately hinders you from going further in the organization.

You may believe that this behavior efficiently focuses your energy on doing what's best for yourself, but in reality it limits your effectiveness and your impact on the organization. You may think that no one will notice what you do; after all, it doesn't seem as if anyone is watching. However, in my experience, people *are* watching, and word gets around. Put another way, justice may not prevail at any one point in time, but it almost always *does* prevail over a long period of time. The truth ultimately comes out.

I have met numerous talented professionals who figure all this out only after they have done lasting damage to their reputation and careers. They may not realize the damage they've done until they get a poor review, get passed over for a promotion, or realize they have lost credibility and respect within their organization.

The Power of an Ownership Mind-Set

An ownership mind-set is a powerful tool in reaching your potential. It's challenging because it requires you to believe that justice and fairness will ultimately prevail. This is a leap that only you can make. If you are game to make this leap, here are several specific examples of actions you could take:

- Helping others without regard to what's in it for you. This means seeing your job description as including helping those around you improve their performance.

- Learning to give credit to others. This requires confidence and overcoming insecurities that push you to grab credit for yourself. It also requires you to realize that making others look good often helps you look good.

- Judging your actions through the prism of whether it's good for the organization versus only good for yourself. At most good companies, these two outcomes will tend to be congruent.

- Doing your job with "the next job up" in mind versus the "next job down." This means defining your job broadly to take into consideration the challenges faced by your boss, and even his boss.

Perhaps this sounds overly idealistic, but believe me, it isn't. I have observed numerous situations in which this mind-set has helped transform otherwise strong individuals into invaluable leaders. Similarly, this mind-set has made otherwise solid companies into superb organizations that changed the world. It might be tough to see this essential ingredient from the outside because it doesn't show up in the financial statements or in other metrics. However, smart leaders know it's vital. It is often referred to in discussions of an organization's culture—a key differentiator in companies and in careers.

Of course you must use appropriate judgment in following this advice. For example, you may not want to disagree with your boss in a meeting. (It may be more appropriate to express your views to the boss one on one after the meeting ends.) Fair enough. Whatever tactics you use, you must explicitly decide what approach you want to take when it comes to acting like an owner.

Are you willing to do this? I urge you to come to grips with your view and make a conscious decision. It could be the intangible ingredient that will help you go the extra mile.

Playing with a Degree of Abandon as the Stakes Get Higher

Let's assume you're willing to act as an owner. To internalize this attitude, it helps to be sufficiently relaxed and authentic so that you assert yourself without being unduly hesitant or fearful.

This is also easier said than done. Let's face it: voicing your opinions, helping others without regard to credit, and defining your job broadly all involve some element of risk. A lot can go wrong when you speak up. People may disagree with you or even think you're stupid. Alternatively, they might wonder who you think you are that you can shoot off your big mouth.

You may not believe that senior people really want to see this type of behavior. If they do, why don't they explicitly ask employees to perform this way? Why do most performance reviews tend to predominantly reflect metrics like revenues and other quantifiable accomplishments? Why does your boss struggle to coach you, or even fail to coach you, on these more qualitative matters?

The decision to be authentic and take risks requires courage. It can be hard to sustain this type of attitude over a career. I have consistently observed professionals who spent the early parts of their careers being themselves at work. They actively disagreed when they had an alternative point of view, they were not afraid to speak up, and they were willing to push back and question authority if they believed a proposed action wasn't in the best interests of the company. Almost without exception, these professionals advanced to bigger roles within their firms.

Then, at some point, something strange happened. They had achieved some success and had saved some money. The stakes in their career got a lot higher. They had a bigger job, were dealing with more-senior people, and were involved in more-consequential decisions. They stopped, looked around, and realized they were operating at a higher plateau—and it began to scare them. Like a sports team that stops playing aggressively once it gets a big lead, they began to play it safe. There just seemed to be so much more to lose.

The Store Manager Begins to Play Not to Lose

The thirty-nine-year-old store manager of a large specialty retailer was at a crossroads. He had joined the company nine years earlier as a merchandise manager in the firm's flagship store in a large Midwestern city. He was an excellent merchant and had a keen eye for developing customer trends. He was particularly good at taking calculated risks in recommending new and innovative merchandise that might meet emerging customer demands. He prided himself on being unafraid to speak up and on pushing his superiors to take risks with new merchandise and vendors.

His ideas didn't always work out, but they were sufficiently insightful to significantly improve the performance of the store. He felt like a rock star at the company and was strongly reinforced for speaking up when others were more hesitant. As he commented to me, "I learned in that job that the important thing wasn't to necessarily be right. It was to have the courage to try new things and speak up to let my opinions be known. Our company needed someone like me to play this role, and my approach encouraged others to do the same."

When the previous store manager took on a bigger role in the company, this merchandise manager was offered the opportunity to become store manager. He jumped at the chance. After all, being store manager was his dream. He also felt it was an excellent fit with his skills and expertise. In his first two years in the job, he learned an enormous amount, and the store continued to perform well despite the ups and downs of the economy.

He visited me in my office on one of his trips to Boston. He explained that he still enjoyed his job but now felt that his career was flattening out. His year-end review was solid, he said, but not like the outstanding reviews he used to receive. He no longer felt like the golden boy of his company.

"It's kind of weird," he remarked. "I have a bigger job, I make more money, and I have more status in my community. So why don't I feel better? I feel like I've become the thing I used to rail against—the complacent store manager looking to play it safe. Now that I'm in the driver's seat, I realize there's a lot more to lose from taking merchandise risks. I worry a lot more. Maybe all this comes with greater accountability?"

I asked him to further discuss the "I worry a lot more" comment.

"Well," he said, "I have a bigger job, a bigger house, and people have higher expectations of me. There's just a lot more to lose." He further explained that he had become more risk averse in a number of ways. Here are examples:

- He was more careful about taking risks with new merchandise choices.

- He didn't disagree as much with his bosses. He was now dealing with the VP who headed up store operations for the whole company. He even talked to the CEO every few weeks. He expressed great "reverence" and admiration for these senior executives—their status, expertise, and points of view.

- He had started spending a lot more of his time thinking about what could go wrong—to the point that he was starting to feel much more anxious. He had asked his physician to prescribe something to help him reduce his level of anxiety. He told me he had been taking this medication for the past year and had also started to see a psychiatrist to talk through some of these worries.

I discussed with him his current approach to saving money. He explained that he actually was saving less money now than when he made a lot less. "Listen," he said, "I need to look and act the part of a successful executive. My wife actually encourages me to spend less. But what is all this hard work for if I can't dramatically improve our lifestyle? I joined the country club, even though I don't play golf—but I figured maybe it's time to learn."

I asked him whether he still loved the business. He said he did. We talked through the skills required of the store manager job and assessed how his skill development matched the job needs. It sounded to me as if this role was a very good fit for him.

I reflected back to him that he appeared to have changed his mind-set. I also noticed what seemed to be a dramatic change in his approach to his career: "Five years ago, you were playing this game with zeal and enthusiasm. You knew things wouldn't always go right, but the downside was manageable. Now, you sound like you're playing scared. You're thinking more about your fear of losing than how you're going to win. The question is, *Why?* Have you put so much pressure on yourself with your spending, and aspirations to be a big man around town, that you're undermining your considerable professional skills?

"This is not the end of your career," I continued. "In fact, you could have a big future in front of you. The real question is, why aren't you acting like it?"

He sat quietly and listened. I suggested that he write down all the things that were worrying him. I encouraged him to review the list and determine which of these concerns related to what others thought, his own concerns about his image, and other extrinsic factors. I also urged him to write down how these worries were impacting his behaviors on the job. Was he still acting on conviction, speaking up, taking appropriate risks, and playing the game with some degree of abandon? "Maybe you're holding the bat too tight," I suggested, resorting to a baseball analogy. "It's hard to swing the bat and hit the ball if you're holding on to the bat for dear life."

All of us are susceptible to this kind of trap. We enjoy some success. Then we start to worry about what could go wrong and begin to obsess about losing what we have. We stop doing many of the things that helped us succeed in the first place.

My advice, again, is to play the game with some degree of abandon. It's great to love your job, but it isn't so great to be in love with your job. It's wise to manage risk, act appropriately, pick your spots, and act in a dignified manner. On the other hand, you don't want to be so careful that you stop speaking up, disagreeing when appropriate, taking calculated risks, and generally letting your natural talents come to the fore. You can't act naturally and allow your great instincts and talents to kick in if you're scared. Fear causes people to unwittingly sabotage their own careers.

Organizing your life more effectively can help reduce the probability of falling into this trap. Save your money. Don't let your ego get too big. If you start feeling you need to play the role of big shot, remember that the big-shot role may take more energy than just doing your job.

As you progress in your career, you need to act more as an owner. As you become more experienced, your opinions and instincts are of higher quality and therefore matter more to your firm. You have more to contribute. Be careful that you're not underperforming in terms of your potential—and bottling up your contributions—by playing not to lose.

Values, Boundaries, and Your Philosophy

There is one last critical element of character and leadership. It involves thinking, in advance, about your values and ethical boundaries. Combining this thinking with actual experience can help you develop a philosophy that can be a guide to your career and your life.[2]

Values

Values guide our lives. They guide our actions and shape who we are. Examples of values include your beliefs regarding these aspects of our lives:

- Hard work

- The importance of family

- The importance of fair play

- Teamwork

- Helping others who are less fortunate

- Contributing to the greater good

You can probably think of several additional examples. They are a product of your family experiences, your education, your religion, and the various role models in your life. Your values evolve over time as a result of your continued learning and experience.

I urge you to write down your values and become explicitly aware of them. There are no right answers, but being more aware of your values will shape how you conduct your career and your life, and with whom you choose to associate. It will also help you recognize those with whom you might prefer not to associate, because they do not share your values.

In my case, values have had a powerful impact on what I have chosen to do professionally, what I have chosen to stop doing professionally, and key decisions I have made relating to nonprofit work. For example, as mentioned earlier, I got involved in Project A.L.S. because I saw a unique opportunity to help find a treatment for this horrible disease. I wanted to help prevent suffering.

An awareness of my values has also fundamentally impacted my choice of friends and other close associates. I knew how I wanted to conduct myself and how I wanted my subordinates and peers to conduct themselves. For example, I always urged subordinates to put themselves in the shoes of their client and give advice that would put the client's interests first. This philosophy helped me look at myself in the mirror every day and live with my choices—even if they differed from the choices made by those around me.

Of course, I have made my share of mistakes. You will also make mistakes and face tough choices. Write down your values, and keep a regular diary of your thoughts. It will help inform your decisions and improve your effectiveness.

Boundaries

Boundaries may be a bit clearer than values. Simply put, these are ethical lines that you promise yourself, in advance, you won't cross.

The act of writing down your boundaries gives you a clearer compass against which to manage what you're doing, with whom you're doing it, and where you're going.

Here are several examples of boundaries:

- I will not kill.

- I will not lie.

- I will not cheat.

- I will not steal.

What's the point of defining boundaries? In my experience, you will inevitably find yourself in a situation in which you feel pressured to cross a boundary or violate one of your core beliefs. It could happen for a variety of reasons. You want to please an intimidating client; your boss puts pressure on you to cross a boundary; or a peer tries to convince you that your boundary shouldn't be a boundary at all. Maybe they tell you everyone else is doing it, and you fear you'll be left behind. Maybe you've made a terrible mistake, you feel embarrassed, and you want to cover it up because you can't bear to admit what you've done. Maybe you don't know how to handle a situation, and—rather than deal with it in a straightforward manner—you decide it would be easier to lie.

The point is that when you're under this type of stress, it is too late to start figuring out what you believe. You need to have considered these issues in advance so that you'll have the presence of mind to slow down or push back. If you haven't considered your boundaries in advance, you're much more likely to get pulled into a decision you'll later regret. You'll realize, after the fact, that you've made a terrible mistake and that you truly do own what you do.

Why Do We Lie?

I have conducted many classes with executives in which we explicitly discuss these issues. Typically, I ask how many of them have an ethical boundary against lying. Most, but not all, hands go up. I then ask how many of them have lied. All hands (including mine) go up. We then discuss what this is about. In particular, we discuss the reasons people lie. The reasons often fill an entire blackboard:

- I didn't want to offend the other person.

- It was a minor matter.

- I was scared.

- I was afraid the other person would get angry with me.

- I was afraid they wouldn't buy the product if I told the truth.

- I was anxious, and—in the heat of the moment—I lied.

- I was under time pressure.

- I acted out of insecurity.

- Ambition got the better of me.

- I told them what I thought they wanted to hear.

Many executives have reported back to me that better understanding their reasons for lying has helped them prepare for the next difficult situation they encounter. It enables them to slow down and think more carefully about their actions. It helps them avoid crossing boundaries they don't want to cross.

Why Write Down Your Values and Boundaries?

Here's why I emphasize this issue. The tough reality is this: you could follow all the advice and do all the difficult work described in this book, and still go off course. One of the primary reasons is that you could make the kind of catastrophic mistake that ruins your reputation or even your entire career. Failing to generate revenue, losing a promotion, or making an honest mistake will not ruin your career. An ethical mistake, by contrast, can ruin your career.

In the final analysis, you cannot escape the fact that you own what you do. Claiming you were following orders will not absolve you from responsibility for your actions.

To repeat what I asserted earlier, inevitably, a situation will arise when you feel under severe pressure to act. You will feel as if there is no time to deliberate. You may be pressured by others, feel highly insecure, feel that you must go along, or feel that you have no choice. At that moment, if you haven't thought about your values, your boundaries, and what you believe in, it will be too late to start. You will get swept along—either by others or by your own fears. In that moment, you may make a decision that you will regret for the rest of your life. This is how it happens—that quickly.

If you have thought in advance about who you are and what you believe, you will be more likely to have the strength to slow down, push back, ask questions, seek advice and counsel from others, and—most likely—make a much better decision. Thinking these issues through in advance won't tell you what to decide, but it will cause you to be more aware that you're about to cross a boundary. This awareness, in turn, should help you to take the appropriate steps to make the right judgment.

For better or worse, these types of situations will come up. In a difficult economic environment, they are likely to come up with greater frequency. It is much easier to deal with decisions that pertain to meeting your economic, legal, and ethical responsibilities when your business is growing and making money. These trade-off decisions get much tougher when you are in a severe economic environment and your business is fighting for survival.

You can inoculate yourself to some extent by having thought about this in advance. As discussed in chapter 4, it also helps to understand who you are. As you will see in the next chapter, it also helps if you build a support group to assist you in thinking through key issues you face.

Character and Leadership

After you've worked through the issues discussed in the first several chapters of this book, character and leadership will help you bring your performance to a higher level. I strongly believe this is the intangible ingredient that makes the difference between being good and being great. Think of the great athletes, musicians, business leaders, government leaders, and so on. Are they really the ones with the most natural talent? Or do they bring to their work an intangible quality that helps them pull together their skills and passions to achieve a higher level of performance?

Character and leadership are key ingredients that pull you to a higher level in whatever endeavor you are pursuing. Consider whether your talents, passions, and approach to the job are enough. Focus on whether your character and leadership need to be improved if you are to reach your true potential.

Suggested Follow-Up Steps

- Think of a person you hold in high esteem as a role model. Write down the elements of his or her behavior that you respect highly. Which of these elements are skill-related and which relate to their character and leadership traits? Give yourself a grade for the degree to which you display these types of behaviors. Write down the factors that impede you and the factors that help you act in this manner.

- Write down the three biggest changes you would like to see made in your project team, business unit, or company. If you were in charge, what specific actions would you take to make these changes? Have you voiced any of these suggestions to your boss in a constructive manner?

- Think about what keeps you from speaking up at work. Write down these impediments, and discuss them with friends and loved ones.

- Write down your values. Write down ethical boundaries that you promise yourself you will not cross. Discuss these values and boundaries with friends and loved ones.

CHAPTER SEVEN

The Importance of Relationships

You Can't Do This Alone

- Do you have a small group of people who care enough about you to tell you things you may not want to hear but need to hear?
- Do you cultivate people with whom you can discuss your various types of support needs?
- Do you provide support and counsel to others?
- Do your relationships evolve over time as your career and life change?

Your ability to take many of the actions recommended in this book will be greatly enhanced if you are able to develop mutually beneficial relationships. One of the biggest impediments to reaching your potential is isolation. It's not a lack of skills or bad luck that sets you back; it is that you become isolated and lose perspective. You don't see yourself objectively, your blind spots get bigger, and you make poor decisions because you fail to assess things clearly. All of us are susceptible to backing ourselves into a corner and perceiving the world (and ourselves) in a distorted way. Relationships help you punch through this isolation.

You may be thinking that it's never been easier to develop relationships. We have an entire generation that is now connected in a myriad of ways: hundreds of friends on Facebook, lots of followers on Twitter, and numerous professional associations on LinkedIn. Heck, you probably get dozens or even hundreds of text messages and e-mails a day. You don't have a problem connecting and interacting with people. If anything, you have an embarrassment of riches.

However, these types of relationship indicators can be highly deceiving. Being connected is not the same thing as having real relationships that you can draw on in times of need. You have to be able to sit down with one or two people with whom you can speak openly and honestly about substantive issues.

On the Verge of an Ethical Lapse

A former student of mine was recently married and off to a good start in an excellent job. When he was at school, he had been an excellent student as well as a leader among his classmates. He was in town to recruit for his firm, and he came by my office to say hello.

After we caught up for a few minutes, there was an uncomfortable silence. I asked him if everything was OK.

He said, "Great, fine. Things really couldn't be better." He then launched into a hypothetical question about what he should do in the future if he ever faced a certain type of ethical dilemma.

I pressed him as to why he was asking me this. "What's really on your mind? I mean, what's going on?"

Tears welled up in his eyes. He started to apologize for being emotional. He said he had just wanted to come by to say hello and catch me up on what he was doing. He wasn't sure why he was getting upset.

"No need for apologies," I said. "You can discuss whatever you want to in this office. No pressure, but if you want to tell me what's really on your mind, I'd love to hear it."

"This is going to take more than a few minutes." He proceeded to tell me about a difficult situation he was involved in at work. He had been strongly encouraged by his boss to take an action that wasn't technically illegal but certainly wasn't consistent with his own values and ethical boundaries. He hadn't done it yet but was on the verge of doing so. He had also been encouraged by his boss to withhold information about this situation from others at his company.

Having seen this type of situation before, I asked him, "Who have you discussed this with?"

"No one," he replied.

"Not even your wife, parents, other loved ones, or friends?" I asked. "Literally, you've talked to *no one*? Why?"

He explained that he felt extremely embarrassed about the situation. He didn't tell his wife because he didn't think she would understand, and he didn't want to worry her. He had a couple of close friends, but he didn't think they'd understand either. His parents would definitely not understand. He was close with members of the clergy from his hometown, but he didn't try talking to them because he thought they wouldn't understand his business or comprehend what it was like to work in his firm.

He was alone and isolated. He had not intended to speak to me about this, but as he sat in my office he'd backed into telling me his story. We spent the next hour discussing the situation, and together we developed a potential action plan. He was not yet in a career-threatening situation, but if he did what his boss had asked him to do, he might do irrevocable harm to himself and his career.

He had felt trapped, believing that there was no viable alternative to capitulating. Now, after discussing the problem, he realized he had several choices. He could speak up to (and push back on) his boss, he could speak to senior people at the firm, or he could resign. Whatever action he took, he realized he had to take greater control of the situation. He also realized these types of situations were likely to come up again in the future, and he had to learn how to deal with them so that they didn't become a danger to his career, his reputation, and his overall well-being. In the last part of the meeting, we discussed the need for him to learn to discuss these matters with others (possibly his wife, loved ones, friends, and colleagues) to avoid losing perspective on any given situation.

This story is typical. People at all organizational levels, in all careers and all walks of life, often feel alone and isolated. It is difficult for them to recognize that they may have several viable alternatives. A person on the outside looking in might be able to help them gain some emotional distance and help them recognize that they are not trapped.

Why don't people ask for help or advice more frequently? Very often, they believe that no one will understand what they're going through. They don't want to bother their friends and family with what they perceive as silly little issues. They feel embarrassed to discuss what they're feeling or fearing. This isolation often leads to poor decisions, lost opportunities, and underperformance. Promising careers are damaged, and valuable potential is wasted.

The purpose of this chapter is to discuss how to build relationships that can help you break through the isolation you may feel. We will discuss types of support and advice that you will likely need from others, as well as the types of people you should consider seeking out as part of your support group. The chapter also discusses the impediments you must overcome to develop these types of relationships.

I suggest a few exercises that may help you in this effort. Finally, this chapter discusses the need to update and evolve this effort over time—as you change, your circumstances change, and the world changes.

What Is a Relationship?

In many cases, when we discuss "relationships," our minds go to dating and romantic relationships. You may associate relationships with deep emotional attachment, or at least some level of affection. You may think that a relationship has more to do with your feelings than your intellect.

If you're a seasoned businessperson, the word "relationship" may invoke images of clients or customers—maybe the depositor who has had a checking account with your bank for the past twenty years, or the do-it-yourself homeowner who comes into your hardware store regularly. In my neighborhood in New York, I think of the people who work at the corner diner, where they know my order before I sit down.

Yes, these are all different kinds of relationships. However, in this chapter, I am a bit more clinical in my use of this term. I have learned that a beneficial relationship requires three things: mutual understanding, trust, and respect. Creating this type of relationship is likely to require time, face-to-face interaction, and hard work. It also requires a mix of inquiry, self-disclosure, and candor.

With this definition in mind, make a list of your relationships that have these attributes. If you're like most of us, you may be surprised by who is on the list and who is not.

Why do some people not make it to your list? Maybe you don't trust them; maybe they're indiscreet, and you aren't willing to confide in them. Maybe you simply don't understand the person. Maybe you understand the person, but you don't respect him or her.

On the other hand, you might be surprised that you have this type of relationship with people for whom you don't feel any affection. You might think that emotional attachment or affection is supposed to be present in relationships. Not necessarily. In fact, ask yourself: would you rather like your boss or understand, trust, and respect him or her?

How do you create relationships that have these features—mutual understanding, trust, and respect? I suggest you have to do three things:

- Self-disclose. Tell the other person information about yourself that will help him or her fundamentally understand you better.[1]

- Inquire. Ask questions of the other person to help you understand him or her better.

- Solicit advice. Be willing to ask for constructive advice on matters of importance to you (and be willing to give advice to the other person). In particular, be willing to seek their advice regarding how you could address an area of self-doubt or insecurity.

The Rain in Spain

The CEO of a small company in Madrid came to visit me. He was enrolled in an executive education program at HBS and wanted to discuss his leadership style. He complained that he often heard about bad news too late. "My people come to me with problems only after it is too late to do something constructive to address them," he explained. "I keep telling them they have to come to me sooner, but they still wait too long. What do I do? Maybe I've got the wrong people working for me?"

I asked him about his relationships with his direct reports, and he said that those relationships were very strong.

"Yet your people delay in disclosing bad news and problems to you?" I asked.

"Well, yes, they do," he acknowledged. "But that doesn't mean we don't have good relationships. I like each of them very much, and I think they like me."

"Have they met your wife and family?" I asked.

No, he said, mainly because there hadn't been a company event where the opportunity presented itself.

I asked if they knew about his background, education, interests, and so on.

"I'm not sure," he said. "Do they *need* to know that?"

"Yes, it might make a big difference," I said. Then I asked him, "What do they know about you that would help them understand you better? Do they know how many kids you have? Do they know your likes, dislikes, and interests? Do they know what keeps you up at night?"

He stopped and thought for a few minutes. "No, I don't think I've ever gotten into that type of conversation with them. Do you think that would be a good idea?"

Before answering, I asked if he ever sought their advice on matters that were worrying him.

Again, he thought about it. "No," he finally said, "I don't usually seek their advice. Generally, I first decide what we ought to do, and then I speak with them about it. Sometimes I do ask them for tactical advice regarding how we should execute one strategy or another—is that what you mean?"

I suggested his job might be a whole lot easier if he had better relationships with his employees.

"Maybe I don't know what you mean by the term 'relationship,'" he said, "because I thought I had good relationships."

"Why do you think someone would come to you with bad news when you're not willing to disclose to them even basic information about yourself?" I asked.

It's not easy to raise bad news with the boss—it requires trusting and understanding the boss—and he hadn't taken even the most basic steps to develop that type of mutual understanding. If he didn't trust them enough to reveal some aspects of his life, share his deeply held concerns, and get their advice on significant issues, why should he expect them to trust him enough to bring him bad news early?

He absorbed this for a few minutes. He hadn't thought about relationships in this way. He thanked me for my time and left my office, and I didn't hear from him again until he sent me an e-mail eight months later. "You probably don't remember all the details of our conversation in your office," he wrote. "You gave me great advice, and I followed it. It has made a world of difference in my company and in my effectiveness. I just wanted to tell you and thank you."

Of course, I got a kick out of the message, but I'm not telling this story to pat myself on the back. Instead, I want to demonstrate how a few simple relationship building steps can help you improve your job performance.

Try Building Your Relationship Muscles

If you don't believe me—or even if you do—try the following simple exercise. It will take about fifteen minutes and will require you to team up with another person.

Step 1. Write down something fundamental about yourself that the other person doesn't know. This information should be something that would help that person to understand you better. Your discussion partner should do the same thing.

Step 2. Share with each other what you wrote down.

Step 3. Write down a question that, if answered, would help you understand the other person better.

Step 4. Ask and answer each other's question. Do not interrupt each other.

Step 5. Write down an area of concern or self-doubt—for example, "I'm not very good at _____."

Step 6. Disclose that self-doubt or concern to the other person, and ask for advice on how you might address it. The other person should, in turn, do the same with you.

What did you learn from performing these steps? I have done this exercise with thousands of students and executives. Initially, before we start the exercise, they think it sounds a bit silly. After we've finished, fifteen minutes later, they recognize the power of these simple steps. Even among seasoned executive teams whose members have known each other for many years, individuals often comment, "This is the best conversation I've ever had with this person. I understand them much better. I wish I had taken these steps years ago."

Think about your relationships. Think about how often you commit time and energy to executing these three relationship-building tasks. Try to incorporate this discipline into your life and work relationships.

The Mode Matters

One other key element you must consider is your choice of communication mode and setting. Your choices here are likely to have a critical impact on your ability to build relationships.

Certain kinds of conversations tend to go far better if conducted in person rather than by phone. In person, I can see my counterpart's facial expressions and body language (and that person can observe mine). For highly critical relationships and sensitive communication, in person is much less risky than the telephone. I've found that occasionally a telephone discussion might go very poorly, whereas the same discussion in person might have gone very well.

In addition, I've learned the power of one-on-one communication versus group discussions. For example, if I want to receive direct feedback (or want to give direct feedback), it is better to do it in person and one-to-one. No one wants to give or receive criticism in front of others—and you can easily damage a relationship by failing to meet the other person individually when you're discussing a sensitive matter.

Numerous new options exist for communicating a message—for example, e-mail, text messages, and cell phone calls, along with the traditional options. I often see people make poor choices regarding which of these modes to use, and as a result, damage their working relationships.

Struggling with Client Relationships

I recently met with a salesperson who uses e-mail extensively to communicate. He was lamenting his struggles to get closer to potential clients and colleagues. After reviewing his communication patterns, he realized he was overusing e-mail. He realized this mode is more suitable for simple messages, updates, and postings. It can be woefully inadequate for communicating complex ideas or nuances.

For example, using humor, irony, or sarcasm in e-mails can be perilous. This salesperson told a story of inadvertently offending one of his important clients because the client misinterpreted one of his well-intended efforts to be funny via e-mail.

He realized that to be clearly understood he needed to let his clients observe his verbal cues and body language. It was just as critical that he have the opportunity to observe them. He learned that using e-mail, when another mode is more appropriate, can lead to serious misunderstandings.

Consider whether a phone call would be more effective than an e-mail; consider a landline phone call before using your cell phone; consider an in-person meeting when mutual understanding is critical; and find a comfortable, quiet, and confidential venue if the conversation is highly sensitive. Of course, in all cases, you should also consider blocking out time in advance and picking a setting that allows each of you to focus and talk uninterrupted.

Think about these choices before you have a discussion you believe is critical to initiating, building, or maintaining an important relationship. Consistently making poor communication mode choices can sabotage your ability to develop strong relationships.

Being Aware of Your Support Needs

Each of us has a variety of relationship needs. They vary by time, situation, and circumstance. We are all unique in this regard. Figuring out your needs requires you to understand yourself and also the types of interactions that might help you gain clarity on certain issues you face. Start by making a list of your various needs. I will share some of mine:

- Love

- Reassurance

- Encouragement

- Praise and positive reinforcement

- Advice

- Constructive criticism and coaching

- Building faith and hope in the unseen (which may be as simple as helping you feel that everything is going to somehow work out OK)

- Intellectual stimulation

Most of us (including me) never take the time to list our needs. In certain situations and at certain times, we may know we feel lousy, but we aren't sure why. We may know that we have needs—emotional or otherwise—that demand attention, but we don't really think much about them at any given moment.

As you make the list, you may be surprised at what pops out. Be aware that it may vary depending on what's happening with you. For example, if you're sick, you're likely to have certain kinds of relationship needs—maybe sympathy and attention, at least until you feel better. In an economic downturn, you may have other relationship needs—maybe reassurance and advice about how to navigate through a difficult period.

Try to add some analytical rigor to these questions. Drill down, and try to put your finger on the pulse of what might be bothering you. A classic case arises when you are beginning to feel dissatisfied with your job and starting to think about quitting. Can you go back to your list of needs and determine which of them aren't being met?

I Think I Want to Quit

I was recently approached by a friend who was running an entrepreneurial venture with a partner. The two of them had built an excellent retail business over five years, and they had a good reputation and a strong following in Southern California. Now my friend was thinking about quitting and was beginning to consider a return to graduate school to earn an advanced degree. I was surprised because I knew her professionally and had always believed she loved her work. In particular, she had keen fashion and design talents. She had worked for many years to get into a position to run this business and now seemed to be thriving—or so I thought.

She asked me what I thought about her plan. I responded that I was shocked to hear she was going to give up her business. When I asked her what she planned to study in school, she said she hadn't yet made up her mind, but she mentioned a couple of fields that might interest her. She also told me her husband was supportive of whatever she wanted to do.

"What happened?" I asked. "I thought you loved this job and things were going really well."

She was surprised that *I* was surprised.

I took a different tack. "OK," I said, "if you could do anything you wanted to do, what would it be?"

She thought for a minute and then smiled. "Well, my knee-jerk answer would be to describe what I'm doing right now—my current business."

"So what's going on?"

She thought about it and then started to talk about her relationship with her partner. They were disagreeing more frequently on key decisions. As a result, the job had become more stressful. She began to dread going to work. In addition, the economic environment meant they had been compelled to make tough choices and, given their strained relationship, it was getting tougher and tougher. "I need harmony and reassurance," she explained. "I can't stand conflict. Also, if I want to do something, I don't want to be told why I can't do it. I want someone who will talk it through with me and work constructively with me. I'm not getting what I need from this relationship, and that's probably why I'm thinking about quitting."

"Are you able to somehow discuss all this with your partner?" I asked.

She admitted they had not discussed these issues. They had been close friends for twenty years, and so each assumed she knew what the other was thinking. As a result, they hadn't taken the time to step back and get reacquainted in this new context.

I offered my two cents of advice: "Before you blow up this great thing you've built—and you still seem to love—try to work on your relationship with your partner." I described the process of self-disclosure and recommended they try it. "Then ask her some questions about what's she's thinking and feeling, and give each other some advice on how to deal with each other."

She reported back after a few weeks. They had had some great discussions, which they thoroughly enjoyed. These talks reminded her why she had gone into business with her partner in the first place. Over the years, though, they had stopped thinking about their individual needs and stopped working on the relationship.

Ultimately, they agreed to divide their responsibilities differently. Until this point, they had done many tasks together. They realized this not only was inefficient but also was creating friction between them. They also decided to create a quarterly "time-out" day, in which they do self-disclosure, inquiry, and advice-seeking in a structured manner.

Today, with this new arrangement, they are back at work and doing well.

Creating Supportive Relationships

Of course, not all of our needs can be met by one person—as much as we may want to try to make it so. My colleague Bill George speaks extensively about the importance of a support group.[2] This is made up of several people with whom you individually cultivate and build relationships over the years. They may never actually meet each other, but each individual has the potential to be helpful in certain types of situations. The reason to develop this group now is that you can't always anticipate what type of help and advice you're going to need. If you are highly isolated and have few close relationships, you are likely to find it very awkward to approach someone you really don't know to seek advice and counsel, particularly if you're in the middle of a crisis.

Begin by listing types of people with whom you'd like to build strong relationships. I'll throw out a few of mine:

- Clergy

- Trusted friend

- Spouse or other loved one

- "Wise" person—someone with experience and good judgment who knows you (for example, a teacher)

- Expert (lawyer, doctor, financial expert, architect, etc.)

- Direct boss, other superiors at work, peers at work

- Work subordinates—in particular, direct reports

Being systematic about making this list should prove useful to you. For example, it may highlight gaping holes in your existing relationships. If you feel isolated in certain types of situations, identifying these holes may help you figure out why.

Write down both your current list of relationships and your aspirational list, and compare the two. Where are the obvious gaps? Are there actions you could take to fill the gaps? Again, you're not looking to make best friends or find folks to go to the movies or dinner with (although that could be an unintended by-product). These are relationships from which you hope to draw advice, emotional support, and counsel. At the same time, these are people for whom you would be prepared to offer this type of support. They are people with whom you would be willing to work to build mutual understanding, respect, and trust.

Again, even though this handful of people may be referred to as a support group, it may never actually meet as a group. Its various members may not even know each other. It is a series of individual relationships, drawn upon as needed. Yes, you may decide to meet with a subset as a group, but the main purpose here is to develop strong individual relationships. Creating an initial list is worth effort and careful thought because it will likely take a concerted effort to build enduring and mutually beneficial relationships.

Identifying the Gaps

After doing this analysis, you may want to step back and analyze the types of gaps you see. There may be a pattern that requires deeper thought. All of us have gaps in our relationships. Let's look at a few examples.

Gaps Due to Problems at Home

We have to go to work every day, even when we're having relationship problems with our spouse or children. This type of strain makes it hard to focus on work, clouds our perceptions, and causes us to react to annoyances in an exaggerated way.

In this situation, it's great if you have relationships with coworkers or others outside work in whom you can confide and who can help you manage yourself through this situation. It may make sense to seek the help of a professional. In any event, it's tough to work through this all by yourself.

No Relationships at Work

Some people have strong and diverse relationships outside work, but they have decided they don't want to have strong relationships at work. With this mind-set, they disclose very little about their lives, inquire very little of others about their lives, and are not well positioned to seek advice at work if they need it. They may say they have mentors outside work, but they are often surprised by criticisms they receive at work that the mentor never raised—or in some cases disagrees with.

The problem with this approach is that you spend a substantial portion of your waking hours at work or dealing with work-related matters. Consequently, your ability to develop your skills, understand your passions, match your skills to the job, and exhibit character and leadership qualities—and even understand who you are—are all likely to be enhanced significantly by feedback and advice you receive from coworkers (seniors, peers, or subordinates). You need relationships with people at work if you're going to reach your potential.

Relationships Only at Work

Many young people decide they're going to work around the clock during their early career to establish themselves. They may have a boyfriend, girlfriend, or spouse, but otherwise they don't focus on establishing non-work relationships. As some have commented to me, in so many words, "I only have twenty-four hours in a day, and if I'm going to have relationships, it's easier to have them with people at my company."

The problem with this approach is that it winds up creating a different type of isolation, in which you see everything from the perspective of the company. What's important to the company becomes what's important to you. This situation causes some people to rationalize otherwise unacceptable or questionable behaviors because these behaviors seem to be prevalent at the company. It is tough to push back against questionable behavior, gain perspective, and exhibit leadership if your relationships are primarily at your job.

This is another reason—as I argue in chapter 2—that non-profit and other community activities can be critical to your development. You don't want to become so isolated that the company starts to feel like your entire world. I have seen many talented professionals atrophy, in their judgment and skills, because they didn't make an effort to build relationships outside work.

I'm Networked and Connected

Another potential approach is to have lots of relationships, lots of connections, and to take every opportunity to meet people. This mind-set is exemplified by the person who walks into the office of a professor or business executive and states, "I want you to be my mentor." Let's imagine that the business executive or faculty member responds by saying, "Sure, I would be glad to help you." The young person feels good he has made a connection, but neither party knows exactly what to do next. Unfortunately, although this approach may feel good from a quantity point of view, it's not good from a depth-and-quality standpoint.

This exercise should not be about quantity. The truth is, if you have five or six strong relationships to call on, you're very fortunate. Those relationships take time, consistency, and mutual effort to build and sustain. They are developed one at a time, and not in clumps. They require focus. Networking has its uses, but it is not a substitute for real relationships—the kind you can count on when it's crunch time.

Impediments to Seeking Support

I've recounted several stories in which people came to me for advice and told me they'd spoken with no one about their situation. The good news is they did ultimately decide to go to someone for advice; the bad news is they waited so long that an initially manageable issue had become an ominous iceberg. Why didn't they reach out sooner?

There are lots of reasons. They didn't want to bother anyone. They didn't think others would understand. They didn't have a person they trusted or respected enough to confide in. They feared that the person in whom they confided would no longer respect them.

To help deal with the myriad of objections you might throw out to justify why you don't go for advice and support to others, try the following exercise.

Think of a time when someone approached you for help, support, or advice, and—as it turned out—you were immensely helpful to that person. You were great.

Do you have that scenario in mind? Now ask yourself the following questions:

- How did you feel? How did it make you feel to be asked for advice?

- What was the mode of communication the other person used to solicit your advice—in person, phone, e-mail, letter, or some other mode? How did the mode they chose impact the quality of your interaction?

- What did you do that was helpful?

- What did you learn about yourself as a result of this interaction?

I have conducted this exercise with students and executives for years. Invariably, people smile to themselves when they recollect the situation and write down the answers to these questions.

Why are they smiling? They realize they were enormously flattered to be asked their opinion. They also realize that the most effective interactions were face-to-face. Sometimes they simply listened to the other person, sometimes they asked good questions, and sometimes they offered their own opinions. In almost all cases, they learned about themselves through this interaction. Most important, this recollection helps them to realize that people want to have relationships and want to help if you're willing to approach them and make the effort.

What to Do Next?

Think of situations when you wished you had reached out to someone for advice and support. Write down the reasons you did not reach out. Now ask yourself: What did you lose? What was the cost of not reaching out?

Go back and think about your list of support needs and your list of potential candidates with whom you might be able to build mutually supportive relationships.

Read other publications that deal with this topic. In particular, I recommend Bill George's book *True North*.

Relationships Evolve Over Time

The challenge with relationships is that things are always changing.

Your job changes, you change, your relationships change, your needs change, and so forth. As a result, relationship development can't be a static or one-time exercise. To reach your potential, you're likely to develop relationships continuously. Think of relationship development as a skill you want to cultivate.

A highly successful brand manager moved with his family from London to Frankfurt, Germany. The move was part of a big promotion. Although he and his wife had traveled to Germany several times over the years, they didn't speak

German. They kept their house in London, rented an apartment in Frankfurt, and put their two children in an international school. The brand manager took a language course for several months before beginning the assignment, and he felt he had a rudimentary grasp of German. He came to HBS as part of an executive program and one day visited me to discuss his job.

I asked him how it was going. "It's been rough," he answered. "My wife feels isolated at home and hasn't been able to make friends. I've made some friends at work, but it has been somewhat superficial. We've been going to London on most weekends and staying with my wife's family, so we haven't really been around on weekends to socialize very much. Several German couples have invited us out, but we just haven't found the time to go out with them yet. I spend almost all my time working, so we haven't really met folks in the community. We go to church most Sundays in London, so we can't meet people in Frankfurt that way. I've got three years to go on this assignment, and I'm not sure we're going to make it."

I sympathized with him. I was sent to Japan by my firm in the early 1990s—a point in my life when I wasn't mature enough or skilled enough to develop a range of mutually beneficial relationships. As a result, I struggled at many points to perform at my best and keep perspective.

I asked him to list his relationships, including those in Germany. He named a large group of people in London and even a few in Asia, where he was once stationed. Tellingly, he couldn't name anyone in Frankfurt.

"Why not?" I asked. He admitted he just hadn't made it a priority.

I didn't have a lot to say other than the obvious: he needed to make it a priority. This probably meant spending some weekends in Frankfurt and allowing himself, his wife, and their children to become part of the community. "You're going to run out of gas, otherwise," I told him. "And it's not surprising. These assignments require more emphasis on relationship development. Most of us fail to adequately focus on this."

An overseas assignment is particularly challenging in terms of developing relationships and maintaining a support group. But, in fact, it's simply a distilled version of the challenge we all face when we change cities, countries, or jobs. The truth is that we all must work at this—and it's a never-ending process.

Relationships Are Essential for You to Reach Your Potential

You can't do this alone.

You can *try* to go it alone, and for a period of time it may even seem to be working—but my own experience, and the experience of all those with whom I've worked over the years, tells me that reaching your potential is dramatically harder if you can't call on relationships at critical junctures. Every prescription in this book is easier to practice if you can put yourself in a position to talk to other people in a mutually trusting and understanding way.

Suggested Follow-Up Steps

- Do the individual exercises described in this chapter.

- Pair with another person, and do the exercise of engaging in self-disclosure, inquiry, and advice-seeking.

- Make a list of issues that concern you. Which of them have you discussed with someone else? Push yourself to identify potential relationships within which you could discuss one or more of these issues.

- Write down the last two times you provided advice and support to others. Write down what you learned from these experiences. How might these insights help you further reduce your own isolation?

CHAPTER EIGHT

The Road Map

Bringing It All Together

What I think is, it's never too late . . . or, in my case, too early, to be whoever you want to be . . . There's no time limit, start anytime you want . . . change or stay the same . . . there aren't any rules . . . We can make the best or worst of it . . . I hope you make the best . . . I hope you see things that startle you. Feel things you never felt before. I hope you meet people who have a different point of view. I hope you challenge yourself. I hope you stumble, and pick yourself up. I hope you live the life you wanted to . . . and if you haven't, I hope you start all over again.

—ERIC ROTH, SCREENPLAY, *THE CURIOUS CASE OF BENJAMIN BUTTON*[1]

Building a fulfilling career is a significant challenge. It takes a lot of courage to chart your course and make the necessary changes along the way. A wide variety of factors contributes to the complexity of this challenge. The future is uncertain, and the world keeps changing, and we are constantly receiving well-intentioned advice—often contradictory and even counterproductive—about how to achieve our dreams.

With all this uncertainty, it's often tempting to just do what everyone else is doing. Or is there another way? Are there people who have defied conventional wisdom and peer pressure and carved out a path that fits their unique skills and passions? Is it only a pipe dream—or is it a real possibility?

There Is Another Way

Consider the following short sketches.

An accomplished business school graduate—let's call her Abbigail—chose to work at a venture philanthropy firm in California right out of school. Many of the graduates in her class went into finance or consulting, but Abbigail had a passion for helping start new philanthropic ventures. At the time of her graduation, this was a nascent field, and her classmates scratched their heads at this job choice. Since graduation, she has played a key role in developing more than twenty-five new ventures that are making a significant impact around the world. Her firm has become more visible and prestigious, and her job is now a hot job on campus. She loves what she does and wouldn't want to trade positions with any of her graduate school classmates.

Azim, a plant manager in a Malaysian consumer goods company, dreamed of someday being his own boss. He had an idea for starting a contract manufacturing business, which he believed would fill an important need faced by global consumer goods companies. His friends and family were impressed with his current position and urged him to stay where he was and continue to move up in the organization. Then, after the untimely death of one of his parents, Azim began to believe that life was shorter than he had thought, and his fear of having later regrets began to outweigh his fear of failing. He used his savings and the backing of several venture firms to start a new business. The jury is still out on how profitable the company will become (although it is off to a good start), but as this newly minted entrepreneur comments, "Whatever the outcomes, I am thrilled to be doing a job that makes the most of my capabilities and fulfills my dream." Azim has been surprised to learn that the outcome is less important to him than the journey.

Devon, a college graduate from the Midwest, decided he wanted to go into finance. Devon loved the stock market and had been watching it every day since he was ten years old. His father, a salesman, had taught Devon about the market. He had a passion for analyzing companies and thinking about the markets. His parents were children of the Depression and had hoped their son would go to law school and get a professional degree. To their initial disappointment, he decided to go to work for a money manager. Devon worked there for several years, developed his skills, and then started his own small firm. He now manages money for a number of families and institutions in the Midwest. He loves what he does. It was his dream.

Heather worked in a professional services firm. It was a prestigious job, and she was honored to work at the company. Both her parents were successful lawyers and were proud that their daughter was also in professional services. After a few years, though, Heather realized she didn't have a passion for the key tasks of the job or the mission of the firm. Further, she saw that her performance was starting to erode. After a great deal of thought, she decided that what she loved was helping people with their problems. She had keen insights about people. Even though she was in her early thirties, Heather decided to return to school, take pre-med courses, and attend medical school. Her concerned parents urged her to rethink her decision, but Heather stuck with it and ultimately became a psychiatrist. She helps people every day, and she's one of the happiest people I know.

As a sales manager in a consumer goods company, Jamal always tried to help his peers, even when no one was watching. He enjoyed his job, believed in his company, and felt that helping others was one way he could make an additional contribution. He expected nothing in return. After he had spent several years at the company, the executive VP job became available. Jamal wanted the job, but he understood that other salespeople had been bigger revenue producers. One day his phone rang. It was the CEO offering him the job. The CEO explained that he wanted to create a more teamwork-oriented culture at the company and that Jamal's selfless actions over the years had convinced him Jamal was the right person to be promoted.

As a grade school teacher, Colin volunteered on weekends at a shelter for homeless people. Only his wife knew about this work. It was something that made Colin feel good. After several years of volunteering, he was approached by a board member to see if he would be willing to join the board. He gladly accepted. The board assignment gave him a chance to learn much more about the shelter and also to understand many of the organizational issues involved in running a nonprofit. Colin eventually became chairman of the board and was honored a few years ago for his substantial contribution to the community. He felt a bit sheepish about being honored, but he did love being chairman. Many of the comments from speakers that night reminded Colin that he had a bigger impact than he might have thought. "I realized," he later commented to me, "that maybe I had made it."

Paul, a medical school graduate, decided to pass on a lucrative career in private practice. Instead, Paul realized his passion was global health—in particular, trying to help improve the health of citizens in Haiti, Rwanda, and other countries where people die of diseases that are preventable in more developed countries. Since his graduation, Paul has never made the lucrative income that he could have commanded in private practice. On the other hand, he has achieved an aspiration that was far more important to him: making a significant contribution to improving global health. Along with a like-minded medical school classmate, Paul cofounded a nonprofit dedicated to global health in developing countries. It has improved the health and overall quality of life of millions of citizens in less-developed countries around the world. His passion and great skills have helped attract donors, volunteers, and other like-minded medical practitioners—people who want to make a difference in the lives of others.

I know each of the men and women in these stories, as well as the central players in many other similar stories. These people have had their struggles and moments of doubt. All of them have come to realize that the effort to reach their unique potential is a journey—an ongoing process that yields insights and raises new questions but doesn't have a final destination.

As I was writing this book, I occasionally mentioned the title to one of my friends. They would usually ask me, "So, are *you* doing what you're meant to do? Have you reached *your* potential?"

In response, I would have to say, "No, I'm still working on it. I'm still working on figuring it out. In fact, I'm not sure I'll ever fully reach my potential—at least I *hope* I won't." I hope I will always be working to understand myself, aspire to accomplish new things, dream new dreams, and work to develop my skills so that I can tackle new challenges. I hope I will always want to find a way to make a positive impact on the world and improve myself.

This Book: It's About You

I wrote my first book, *What to Ask the Person in the Mirror*, to help leaders develop their skills and build their organizations.

In that book, I argue that leadership is much more about asking the right questions than having all the answers. You don't need to carry the weight of the world alone on your shoulders—and you don't need to be Superman or Superwoman.

You *do* need to ask key questions and take time to reflect on the answers. In this way, leaders and potential leaders can create and follow a road map to develop their capabilities and steer their organizations successfully. I hope anyone who reads that book will be better equipped to be a leader.

Although I am proud of that book, I knew when I finished it that there was still a big problem left to tackle: there's a difference between knowing the questions you should ask, the skills you need to acquire, and the actions you should take and being able to actually ask those questions, acquire those skills, and perform those tasks.

There is a critical actor who must be understood and managed in this equation: *you*. Are you able to accurately assess your skills? What are your passions? Do you understand who you are? Do you have a dream job in mind? Do you apply your skills and passions to be outstanding in that job? Do you exhibit character and leadership traits? Do you have a support group that you can rely on? All these questions and variables have a powerful impact on your ability to do your job, excel, and achieve your dreams.

There is no one path for doing this. Each of us is unique and brings a range of qualities to any situation. We each progress at our own pace and in our own ways. We each are more likely to excel at certain activities than others. We can't be put into a box and expected to perform.

Given all this, it is ironic that many talented people don't try to understand their own unique qualities. They find it easier to focus on debating intellectual questions rather than understanding themselves well enough to figure out who they are and what they love. It is easier for them to mimic others than to figure out how they can develop themselves to be at their best. That's a challenging assignment. It is much easier to follow the crowd.

This book lays out a road map for reaching your potential. Of course, you must decide whether you want to go down this road.

A Progression

Consider the framework shown in figure 8-1, which is first presented in the introduction to this book.

This progression starts with understanding the rules of the road and then understanding yourself. Then the framework suggests strategies for excelling and ideas for going the extra mile to reach your potential.

Reaching your potential is different from developing strategy for a company. In a company, given enough time, money, and determination, you can change most things. Maybe you can't change the world, but you can adapt your organization to the world. You have the ability to change the skills of a company, its character, and its culture. If you have enough time, resources, and determination, you can alter most of the important variables.

This isn't the case with human beings. In an individual, there are certain things you cannot change, and certain things you can. You must figure out which is which. I am five feet ten

FIGURE 8-1

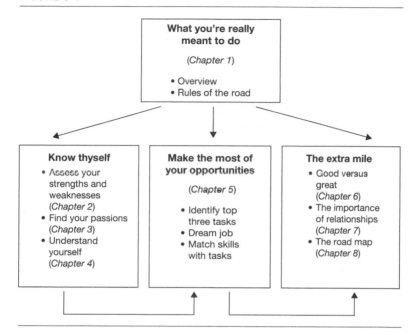

inches tall, and as much as I want to think I'm six feet tall, it's not going to happen. I do sing in the shower, but I would get clobbered if I sang in public. I have strong quantitative and analytical skills, but if I had to teach math or perform a highly quantitative job, I would be in a lot of trouble, no matter how hard I worked.

A frequent mistake made by promising young people is thinking about their lives as if they're developing a strategy for a company. For example, they may believe they're supposed to be able to do whatever their peers can do. If they can't, they're dogged in working to develop those skills so that they can be like their peers. They want to fit in, and they want to compete head-to-head with their peers. The problem is that they don't fully consider the fundamental differences between themselves and those individuals.

A better, but more complicated, path would be for them to assess themselves and determine who they are. This requires first taking an inventory of the skills they currently possess and thinking about which tasks they might enjoy. Based on this assessment, they can then develop a skills strategy to select a profession they want to pursue. This analysis may lead them to work on improving certain weaknesses, building up existing strengths, and selecting an environment that gives them the best opportunity to shine. Over time, and as a result of various experiences, they can update their thinking, refine their interests, and make course adjustments.

Reaching Your Potential

You can follow a systematic process for being at your best. It probably won't be someone else's best; it will be uniquely suited to you. It isn't better or worse than another person's path. It is simply different.

This is a different way of thinking about your career and your life. It will probably involve rejecting conventional wisdom, peer pressure, popular culture, and the like. It may require you to have a thick skin at a cocktail party when you explain why you have chosen to do something you love instead of taking paths similar to those pursued by almost everyone else in the room. Your journey may take years, during which time you may receive little external reinforcement and few accolades. This lack of approval tends to be tough for those who have always been at the top of their class or have been accustomed to judging their progress based on the opinions of others.

Next Steps

I am not starry-eyed about the feasibility of following the prescriptions in this book. I'm not naive about the difficulty of charting your own path. It is hard work and takes fortitude—as I know from personal experience. I am just as susceptible to being swayed by the views of others as anyone else. I like impressing other people. I also know that practical considerations—for example, money—push us to take actions we must take to pay the rent and meet our other obligations. Over the years, I have certainly been swayed by these obligations and worries.

If you choose to follow the framework in this book, here are a few steps that should be useful:

- Keep a journal. You don't need to write in it every day, but make sure to do so whenever you're trying to get clarity on a question. Use this journal as a workbook for the exercises suggested in this book so that you can reflect on your thoughts and observations.

- Read the newspaper every day. Read books and magazines. Stay grounded by keeping up with current events; literature and cultural trends can provide a valuable reality check. Although you don't want to be unduly swayed by popular culture, you do need to be aware of what is going on in the world because the failure to do so can cause isolation. It is also useful to read about how others might be dealing with situations similar to yours.

- If possible, save your money. One of the reasons people fail to reach their potential is the pressure they feel to take care of pressing financial needs. I am not saying that you shouldn't spend your money. I am saying that being overextended makes it terribly difficult to pursue your skills and passions. It also makes it much harder to speak up, push back, and generally do what you believe is right. Saving your money at various points in your career may make it more likely you'll make much more money later. Why? It's because it will allow you to exert a greater degree of leadership and make better career decisions when it counts.

- Build time in to your schedule for vacations and time off. I am regularly approached by people who tell me they haven't taken a vacation in several years. If this is the case, I can see why it's difficult for them to get perspective or reflect. Getting away helps you become sharper and more aware. This book is about self-awareness. If you beat yourself to a pulp, being self-aware will always be a struggle.

- Don't let your relationships slide. All of us—including me—struggle with this. This is why we all need to work hard at maintaining relationships over the long term. I regularly ask for advice. When I say something stupid or get angry, I apologize (a lot). Chances are that you'll be better at this than I am, but you will need to work at it.

- See a professional if it helps. Here I am referring to a psychologist or psychiatrist. Surprisingly, many people balk at this suggestion. For many, there is a stigma associated with seeing a mental health professional. It's not for everyone, but I urge you to consider it if you're struggling to understand yourself. I have seen people battle successfully with anxiety or depression or deal with traumatic events in their lives, thanks to the help of a trained professional. It can make the difference between overcoming hurdles and simply running in place—and no one needs to know about it but you.

Again, these suggestions are meant to help you address the various issues and questions raised in this book.

Bring It All Together

"I wish someone could just tell me what I am really meant to do."

How many times have I heard someone say these words? They are usually spoken by people who are trying to deal with a conflict between their head and their heart. I have felt this way myself on a number of occasions when I just didn't know what I wanted, or I was fearful about the future and anxious about how a decision would pan out. I wanted things to go well, I didn't want to let people down, and I didn't want to have regrets.

Over the years, though, I have learned that regrets and uncertainty are a part of life. You can't avoid them, but you can try to get a better grip on what you can do and who you are. When you reflect on your life, you'll want to feel that you used your talents in a manner that fit your passions and that you have made the type of impact you wanted to make.

What is that impact? As I've said, the answer to this question is different for every individual. Remember, lots of people will tell you what you should do and what you should want, but they don't have to live your life. Chances are, moreover, that they're not very happy with their own lives.

So try a different approach. Worry less about being a success, and worry more about reaching your potential. There are likely to be multiple ways for you to accomplish this, so pick a path that suits you.

One of my favorite quotations is attributed to Albert Einstein: "Not everything that counts can be counted, and not everything that can be counted counts." Of course, metrics are useful—but only to a point. Your definition of success is more likely to be driven by aspects of your life that can't fully be measured or compared with those of your peers. You'll feel it.

If you follow your own path, I don't know how much money you will accumulate, how much stature you will achieve, or how many titles you will garner. But if you're true to your convictions and principles, I know you're far more likely to feel like a big success. In the end, that feeling will make all the difference.

Notes

Introduction

1. Robert Steven Kaplan and Scott Snook, "The Authentic Leader," course syllabus, Harvard Business School, Boston, fall 2011.

2. Bill George with Peter Sims, *True North: Discover Your Authentic Leadership* (San Francisco: Jossey-Bass, 2007).

Chapter Two

1. Laura Morgan Roberts, Gretchen Spreitzer, Jane Dutton, Robert Quinn, Emily Heapy, and Brianna Barker, "How to Play to Your Strengths," *Harvard Business Review*, January 2005, 74–80.

2. Robert Steven Kaplan and Scott Snook, "The Authentic Leader," course syllabus, Harvard Business School, Boston, fall 2011.

Chapter Three

1. Bill George with Peter Sims, *True North: Discover Your Authentic Leadership* (San Francisco: Jossey-Bass, 2007), chapter 6.

2. Laura Morgan Roberts, Gretchen Spreitzer, Jane Dutton, Robert Quinn, Emily Heapy, and Brianna Barker, "How to Play to Your Strengths," *Harvard Business Review*, January 2005, 74–80.

Chapter Four

1. Warren G. Bennis and Robert J. Thomas, "Crucibles of Leadership," *Harvard Business Review*, September 2002, 39–45.

2. Bill George with Peter Sims, *True North: Discover Your Authentic Leadership* (San Francisco: Jossey-Bass, 2007), chapters 1 through 3.

3. Robert Steven Kaplan and Scott Snook, "The Authentic Leader," course syllabus, Harvard Business School, Boston, fall 2011.

4. John Paul Eakin, *Living Autobiographically: How We Create Identity in Narrative* (Ithaca, NY: Cornell University Press, 2008).

Chapter Six

1. Bill George with Peter Sims, *True North: Discover Your Authentic Leadership* (San Francisco: Jossey-Bass, 2007), chapter 5.

2. Ben W. Heineman, Jr., "Avoiding Integrity Landmines," *Harvard Business Review*, April 2007, 100–108.

Chapter Seven

1. Katryn Greene, Valerian J. Derlega, and Alicia Mathews, "Self-Disclosure in Personal Relationships," in *The Cambridge Handbook of Personal Relationships*, ed. Anita L. Vangelisti and Daniel Perlman (Cambridge: Cambridge University Press, 2006).

2. Bill George and Doug Baker, *True North Groups: A Powerful Path to Personal and Leadership Development* (San Francisco: Berrett-Koehler Publishers, 2011); and Bill George with Peter Sims, *True North: Discover Your Authentic Leadership* (San Francisco: Jossey-Bass, 2007), chapter 7.

See also Stephen R. Covey, *The Seven Habits of Highly Effective People: Restoring the Character Ethic* (New York: Simon & Schuster, 1989); David A. Garvin and Michael A. Roberto, "What You Don't Know about Making Decisions," *Harvard Business Review*, November 2001, 108–116; K. E. Kram and M. C. Higgins, "A New Approach to Mentoring: These Days You Need More Than a Single Person. You Need a Network," *Wall Street Journal*, September 2008; Daniel Goleman, "What Makes a Leader?," *Harvard Business Review*, January 2004, 82–91; Roderick M. Kramer, "The Harder They Fall," *Harvard Business Review*, October 2003, 58–66; and John J. Gabarro and Linda A. Hill, "Managing Performance," Case 9-496-022 (Boston: Harvard Business School, 1995).

Chapter Eight

1. Eric Roth, *The Curious Case of Benjamin Button* (screenplay), Paramount Pictures/Warner Bros. Entertainment, 2006 (see http://www.scribd.com/doc/13909016/Curious-Case-of-Benjamin-Button).

Index

Index

Index

Acknowledgments

The ideas and concepts in this book are drawn from a variety of experiences over the past several decades.

I owe a great deal to the numerous mentors, coaches, friends, colleagues, clients, and students whom I have had the privilege to know over these many years. Their wisdom—as well as generosity in sharing their stories and challenges—has been critical to all that I have learned and forms the basis for much of this book.

I had the good fortune to start my career at Goldman Sachs in the early 1980s. The firm and its leaders instilled in me a business philosophy and approach that I was able to test in a variety of leadership positions over twenty-two years. In addition, our superb clients were generous with their time, wisdom, and ideas—well beyond the requirements of professional relationships. Many of the firm's senior leaders served as critical role models in helping me develop my management abilities and leadership skills.

I am enormously grateful to my colleagues at Harvard Business School. They gave me the opportunity to join the faculty in 2005 and have always helped me to become a more effective professor—coaching me to better frame issues, orchestrate effective discussions, and expand my techniques for helping leaders improve their performance. My fellow professors are generous and rigorous thinkers who are intensely interested in understanding the real world and working to improve it. That's a potent combination, and one that has motivated me to further develop my skills and keep learning. I particularly want to thank Bill George for reviewing this manuscript and giving me excellent feedback. In addition, I want to thank my other teaching colleagues—Tom DeLong, Jack Gabarro, Josh Margolis, Nitin Nohria, Leslie Perlow, and Scott Snook—in the course "The Authentic Leader."

My classroom experiences have been hugely influential in shaping this book. Since coming to Harvard, I have had the opportunity to teach a significant number of MBAs and executives at all levels, and that has given me exposure to a wide array of leadership, strategy, and competitive challenges and helped me refine my views regarding human potential. My interactions with executives have taught me a great deal and have provided a laboratory for experimenting with various approaches for improving performance and helping individuals achieve their unique potential.

I want to thank *Harvard Business Review* for giving me the opportunity to write articles on leadership and individual potential. Jeff Kehoe and his colleagues at Harvard Business Review Press—including Erin Brown, Courtney Cashman, Ellen Peebles, and Allison Peter—encouraged me to use those articles as a basis for saying more, and they worked with me at every step to create this book as well as my previous book.

Acknowledgments

I could not have written this book without the help of my editor, Jeff Cruikshank. Jeff is an accomplished author in his own right and has served as a superb coach, mentor, and editor.

I also want to thank Sandy Martin, my fabulous longtime assistant, who puts up with me and makes it possible for me to function efficiently and effectively. Jane Barrett, my assistant at HBS, has been invaluable and outstanding in all that she does. Both Sandy and Jane have helped to keep this project on track over the past year.

Special thanks to Heather Henriksen for encouraging me to write this book. I also want to thank Alissa Emerson, Michael Diamond, Robin Hazelwood, Arlene Kagan, Wendy Winer, David Winer, and Scott Winer for reading and advising me on this manuscript.

Last and most important, I want to thank my parents and family. They have given me love, support, and understanding at every point in my life. Their philosophy, values, and advice echo in the pages of this book.

About the Author

Robert Steven Kaplan is Senior Associate Dean and the Martin Marshall Professor of Management Practice in Business Administration at Harvard Business School. He is also chairman and a founding partner of Indaba Capital Management LLC, and co-chairman of Draper Richards Kaplan Foundation, a global venture philanthropy firm.

Before joining Harvard in 2005, Kaplan spent twenty-two years in a number of senior leadership positions at Goldman Sachs. He served as vice-chairman of the firm, with oversight responsibility for the global investment banking and investment management divisions. He was also a member of the firm's management committee, chairman of its partnership committee, and chairman of the firm's Pine Street leadership program for developing emerging leaders. Prior to becoming vice-chairman, he also served as co-head of global investment banking, head of the corporate finance department, and head of Asia-Pacific investment banking (headquartered in Tokyo). He became partner of the firm in 1990 and today remains a senior director.

Throughout his career, Kaplan has worked extensively with nonprofit and community organizations. He was the founding co-chairman of the Harvard NeuroDiscovery Center Advisory Board. He is co-chairman of Project A.L.S. and founding co-chairman of the TEAK Fellowship. He serves on the board of the Ford Foundation. He also is co-chairman of the executive committee for Harvard University's Office of Sustainability as well as a member of the boards of Harvard Medical School and Harvard Management Company (serving as interim president and CEO from November 2007 to June 2008).

Kaplan was appointed by the governor of Kansas to serve as a member of the Kansas Healthcare Policy Authority Board. He also served as a member of the Capital Markets Advisory Group for the New York Federal Reserve.

Kaplan is a member of the board of the State Street Corporation and chairman of the Investment Advisory committee of Google. He also serves in an advisory capacity for a number of other companies. Over his career, Kaplan has advised and worked closely with senior executives in both the for-profit and the not-for-profit sectors. He has also coached a substantial number of professionals in the early and middle stages of their careers.

As a professor of management practice at Harvard Business School, Kaplan has taught a variety of leadership courses in the school's MBA program and has also taught a substantial number of experienced leaders in the executive education programs. He is author of *What to Ask the Person in the Mirror* (Harvard Business Review Press, 2011), a number of Harvard Business School cases regarding leadership, and two highly regarded

Harvard Business Review articles: "What to Ask the Person in the Mirror" and "Reaching Your Potential."

Kaplan grew up in Prairie Village, Kansas, and received his BS from the University of Kansas. He received his MBA from Harvard Business School, where he was a Baker Scholar.